Grammar Works
Teacher's Book

1

Mick Gammidge

CAMBRIDGE
UNIVERSITY PRESS

PUBLISHED BY THE PRESS SYNDICATE OF THE UNIVERSITY OF CAMBRIDGE
The Pitt Building, Trumpington Street, Cambridge, United Kingdom

CAMBRIDGE UNIVERSITY PRESS
The Edinburgh Building, Cambridge CB2 2RU, UK
40 West 20th Street, New York, NY 10011–4211, USA
477 Williamstown Road, Port Melbourne, VIC 3207, Australia
Ruiz de Alarcón 13, 28014 Madrid, Spain
Dock House, The Waterfront, Cape Town 8001, South Africa

http://www.cambridge.org

First published 1998
Reprinted 2002, 2003

Printed in Great Britain at the University Press, Cambridge

ISBN 0 521 55540 X Teacher's Book 1
ISBN 0 521 55542 6 Student's Book 1

Contents

Introduction

Grammar Works 1 provides grammar presentation and practice for young students from beginner level. It is suitable for use in class, for homework or holiday practice. The grammar syllabus covers those language areas generally taught in first year English courses, and which provide a foundation for further study. *Grammar Works 1* introduces around 600 vocabulary items which are recycled throughout the book. The material is flexible and can be used to provide about 28 hours of study if only the Student's Book is used, and up to around 52 hours if all the extra materials and suggestions in the Teacher's Book are also used.

Features of *Grammar Works 1*

Grammar Works 1 contains the following features:

- Grammar is presented in context, focusing on both form and meaning.

- An inductive approach encourages students to work out grammar rules for themselves.

- Full grammar tables and explanations for reference are in the Student's Book.

- Explanations are presented in simple language and grammatical terminology is clearly introduced.

- A carefully structured progression through each unit moves from controlled, supportive practice to freer practice.

- A range of activity types including inductive exercises, personalisation activities and puzzles provides interest and allows for different learning styles.

- A variety of fun, interesting and educational topics maintains motivation.

- Real-world content and (semi-) authentic texts present grammar in a natural and meaningful way.

- Structures and vocabulary are frequently recycled, both within and between units.

- *Check point* units plus optional photocopiable tests assess students' progress every six units.

- Optional photocopiable materials for vocabulary practice are provided in the Teacher's Book for each unit.

- The Teacher's Book contains suggestions for further practice activities.

Student's Book

There are 24 teaching units and four *Check point* assessment units in the Student's Book. Each teaching unit has eight exercises, leading the student through a progression of activities as follows:

- Units begin with a grammar presentation through texts which show the grammar point in use and illustrate its meaning. A task accompanies the presentation; this may focus on general comprehension or draw attention to the grammar area but requires no production of the target grammar.

- An inductive exercise follows, focusing students' attention more directly on the form and/or meaning of the grammar just presented. After completing the inductive exercise, students check their ideas in the Grammar reference section at the back of the book. (In a few units where a second grammar point is covered, there is an extra inductive section.)

- The Grammar reference section gives students clearly laid out rules and explanations. While students are encouraged to complete the inductive section before they refer to the Grammar reference section, they can work back and forth if wished.

- The exercises then progress from highly controlled practice, focusing on form but reinforcing meaning, through freer tasks where linguistic support is gradually withdrawn until students are required to produce language in response to contextualising cues.

- Exercise 7 is a personalisation exercise which allows students to use the new grammar to talk about themselves and their world.

- Each unit ends with a puzzle. The puzzle relies on students' understanding of the grammar area covered in the unit but focuses on problem-solving; it thus introduces an element of fun, and encourages the development of general cognitive skills.

- *Check point* units provide a review of the previous six units. Each *Check point* unit has six assessment exercises which are not inductive, nor is there a puzzle. *Check point* units can be used either as progress tests or simply for further practice. They are useful as diagnostic aids to check students' learning and highlight areas which may need remedial work.

Teacher's Book

The Teacher's Book offers different levels of support for teaching *Grammar Works 1*, including information on the language covered and on how to teach it effectively in class. The Teacher's Book contains the following features:

- Each unit begins with a general description of the grammar point discussing usage, form, pronunciation and potential difficulties for students, as appropriate.

- All the new vocabulary for the unit is listed.

- Answers to exercises and puzzles are given (including answers to photocopiable worksheets).

- Suggestions are given for supplementary activities based around pairwork, groupwork and classwork, with advice on how and when to use these. They are generally more communicative activities than the written exercises in the Student's Book.

- For each of the teaching units, there is a page of photocopiable vocabulary practice. This worksheet can be used for presentation, practice and written record of new words in the unit. Where appropriate, vocabulary sets are extended a little from the Student's Book in these worksheets.

- For each *Check point* unit in the Student's Book, there is a photocopiable worksheet (*Double check!*), which provides further test or practice material for the previous six units.

Using the Student's Book

Presentation texts

All units begin with an illustrated text which clearly presents the form and the meaning of the new grammar area.

It is a good idea to preview the contexts, and in some units specific suggestions are given. You could use various approaches to preview the context, possibly using the mother tongue, for example:

- Ask students what they already know about the general topic area before they see the text.

- Students look at the illustrations accompanying the text and name as many items as they can in English.

- Students look at the type of text and identify its source, e.g. newspaper, text book, comic, etc.

Inductive exercises

Although answers to inductive exercises are provided at the back of the Student's Book, students should be encouraged to see these exercises as a challenge where they work out rules for themselves before checking their ideas at the back of the book. By checking their answers and studying any additional information, students can be sure they are on the right track before proceeding to the main body of exercises for which answers are given only in the Teacher's Book.

Other exercises

More mechanical question and answer exercises can provide useful, confidence-building drill practice where students ask and answer each other in pairs. Pairwork can be used as a general strategy both to extend communication, and to allow students to compare their ideas and thus become more reflective about their learning. You might remind students that they can actually learn from each other.

Personalisation exercises

Personalisation exercises in each unit give students the opportunity to relate the language to their own world and experience. Students' answers will vary and can be used as the basis for a range of follow-up activities, for example:

- Students compare the content of their answers with a partner.

- Students report either their own or their partner's answers back to the class.

- Students take part in class surveys.

Puzzles

The puzzle is intended to be a fun activity and students should not worry if they can't work out the correct answer. You might want to put students in co-operative groups, or set a time limit for solving the puzzle. You could conduct the puzzle as a race between groups. Some puzzles could be used as a model for students to write similar puzzles if they enjoy this kind of activity.

Supplementing the Student's Book

Grammar Works 1 provides essential grammar presentation and practice focusing on both form and meaning. Grammar terminology is introduced gradually from the beginning, and you may wish to ensure that students learn the most useful and important terms as they go along. You can supplement the material in the Student's Book with suggestions from the Teacher's Book and your own ideas to facilitate grammar practice in a full range of language activities. Communicative grammar practice will help develop students' overall communicative competence. Areas to consider include:

Vocabulary

A good vocabulary provides students with the basic building blocks which, in a grammatical framework, allow them to understand and express ideas. Most of the vocabulary in *Grammar Works 1* is introduced in a way which makes its meaning clear, and there are photocopiable, supplementary vocabulary worksheets for each unit in the Teacher's Book. You may wish to extend the vocabulary beyond the 600 or so words presented. There are various ways of doing this, for example:

- Use the illustrations in the Student's Book to teach items which are not named in the materials.

- Supplement the word sets in the presentation texts with other related, common, key vocabulary.

- Where members of common word sets, e.g. colours, numbers, days of the week, food, occur in the materials, use these as an opportunity to recycle or teach other members.

- You could introduce common antonyms or synonyms for words in the material, where they are appropriate to the students' level.

Reading

The exercises in the Student's Book introduce reading materials in various forms. The presentation material includes a variety of text types, e.g. advertisements, magazine articles, text books, comic strips, film review, dialogues, many of which are adapted from authentic sources. You can exploit these texts to develop reading subskills: guessing vocabulary from context; identifying text type; skimming; scanning.

Some of the units contain cloze exercises which develop reading skills related to cohesion/coherence.

The puzzles also usually provide short but intensive texts for reading practice. If students find it difficult to solve a puzzle, you could ask them to translate it into their own language to check detailed comprehension.

Writing

The largest unit of writing students are required to produce in *Grammar Works 1* is the sentence. Within each unit, support is gradually withdrawn so that in personalisation exercises, students are required to generate their own complete sentences.

There are specific suggestions for additional writing activities in the Teacher's Book. You can use group projects and poster work in particular to encourage students to produce written sentences on subjects that you know interest them. These can be ongoing and continuously extended.

Speaking

Pairwork and groupwork will maximise the opportunities for students to practise their spoken English. The Teacher's Book gives guidance on pronunciation features specific to the grammar areas considered. Encourage students to use contracted forms when they speak.

For freer group activities like project work, encourage students to use as much English as they can during the process. You can offer language support but you don't need to be overly concerned about accuracy (or mother tongue use), as this is a chance for students to take risks and develop fluency and confidence; the product (for example, a poster) will provide the accuracy focus.

You can also teach students useful classroom language, *How do I say … in English? What does … mean?* etc.

Listening

Listening, like speaking, is an inevitable part of communicative pair/groupwork, e.g. *Find someone who …* activities. In more routine interactions, such as comparing answers to exercises, the emphasis can be placed on listening by asking students to do these orally without reading their partner's answers.

You can also devise short dictation exercises, recycling the grammar and vocabulary students have learnt so far.

Conclusion

Grammar Works 1 attempts to make the introduction to English grammar study a lively, meaningful and fun experience for young students. It also aims to make grammar teaching varied, innovative and interesting, and I hope that both you and your students enjoy using the materials.

Mick Gammidge

Be affirmative and negative forms
Pronouns *I, you, we, they, she, he, it*

Be: Meaning
The present tense of *be* refers to ongoing states or temporary states in the present.

Form
- Note that in the contracted form, the apostrophe (') substitutes for the missing letter.
- The contraction is almost always used in spoken English except in very formal situations or for emphasis. In written English this is reversed; the full form is generally used except in informal contexts.
- The two forms of contraction (*you aren't / you're not* etc.) are equivalent. Note that the first person contraction *I'm not* does not have an equivalent *I amn't* in standard English (although it exists in dialect).
- Because *be* changes markedly to agree with person, students whose first language allows the dropping of the subject may be tempted to drop the subject/pronoun in English. This is not generally acceptable.

Pronouns: Meaning
The pronouns *I, you* (singular and plural), *we, they* refer to both male and female.

Vocabulary
Adjectives: *beautiful, busy, dirty, expensive, fast, friendly, happy, hot, hungry, ill, new, old, right, short, slow, tall, thirteen, tired, wrong*
Pronouns: *he, I, it, she, they, we, you*
Verbs: *be (am, are, is)*
Adverbs: *here, today*
Other words: *and, hello, no, not, sorry, yes*

▶ *Worksheet A*

Student's Book answers
1b 1 I 2 you 3 she 4 he 5 it 6 we 7 you 8 they 9 they
    10 they
2 I am = I'm   we are = we're
    you are = you're   you are = you're
    he is = he's
    she is = she's   they are = they're
    it is = it's

Classwork suggestion
Tell students they have one minute to exchange greetings (*Hello, I'm X. / Hello, I'm Y.*) with as many of their classmates as possible.

Student's Book answers
3 1 I'm 2 She 3 You 4 They're 5 We 6 It's

Classwork suggestion
Chain round the class. The first student says: *I'm* (name), *I'm* (age), *I'm* (adjective, e.g. *tall*) and then points to the next student and says, *She/He's* (name), *she/he's* (age), *she/he's* (adjective). The second student then repeats this formula, starting with *I'm* (name), etc. and then pointing to the next student, *He/She's* (name), etc. and so on.

Student's Book answers
4a 's not   're not

b I: 'm not, am not
    she, he, it: 's not, isn't, is not
    we, you, they: aren't, 're not, are not

Classwork suggestion
Write a list of various contracted forms on the board (e.g. 1 *you aren't*, 2 *I'm not*, etc.) and ask students to write down the letter the
▶ *Worksheet B, C and D* apostrophe is substituting for.

Student's Book answers
5 1 ✗ 2 ✗ 3 ✗ 4 ✗ 5 ✓ 6 ✗ 7 ✗
6 1 It isn't fast. It's slow.
    2 He's happy.
    3 They aren't old. They're young.
    4 They're hot.
    6 She's tired.
    7 They're busy.
7 Answers will vary.

Puzzle
Eric is right. (If Linda is right, then Mark is also right in saying Eric is wrong. But only one person is right, so it must be Eric.)

Worksheet

Extra vocabulary: *clean, sad, young*

A Use this activity as a preview to the unit. Preteach the adjectives; mime is a good idea. Students can take it in turns to mime an adjective while partners guess the adjective. They then do the activity for consolidation and written record.

B, C and D Use these activities to introduce and practise the vocabulary before exercise 5. Encourage students to look at the pictures in activity C and think of suitable adjectives before attempting the jumbled words in activity B. For words they don't know, encourage them to use dictionaries.

Answers
B 1 tall 2 clean 3 fast 4 dirty 5 short 6 new 7 slow
    8 old
C 1 He's short. 2 It's new. 3 It's clean. 4 It's fast.
    5 They're dirty. 6 They're tall. 7 It's slow. 8 It's old.
D 1–6 2–8 3–5 4–7

A Draw the faces.

1 She's young. **2** He's sad. **3** He's happy. **4** She's ill.

5 She's old. **6** He's hot. **7** She's tired. **8** He's dirty.

B Move the letters and make words. (Look at the pictures in activity C for help!)

1 l a l t ____tall____   **2** a n e l c _____   **3** s t a f _____   **4** t r i d y _____

5 t h r o s _____   **6** w e n _____   **7** w o l s _____   **8** l o d _____

C Put the words in activity B with the pictures.

1 He's ☐☐☐☐☐.   **2** It's ☐☐☐.   **3** It's ☐☐☐☐☐.   **4** It's ☐☐☐☐.

•   •   •   •

•   •   •   •

5 They're ☐☐☐☐☐.   **6** They're ☐t☐ ☐a☐ ☐l☐ ☐l☐.   **7** It's ☐☐☐☐.   **8** It's ☐☐☐.

D Match and join the opposites in activity C.

2 Who are you?

Be questions and short answers
Who + be ... ?

Form
In questions with *be*, the subject and *be* change places. When *who* is used, the question word is placed at the beginning of the question.

Vocabulary
Adjectives: *brave, British, clever, crazy, fourteen, strong, stupid*
Nouns: *boy, cat, girl, lion, spider*
Pronoun: *who*

Student's Book answers
1b Are you OK?
  Who is she?
2

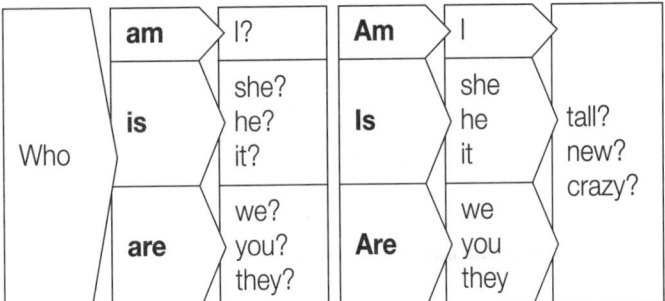

▶ **Worksheet A and B**
Student's Book answers
3 1 Is Lion Boy strong?
  2 Is Spider Boy crazy?
  3 Is Cat Girl brave?
  4 Are Spider Boy and Cat Girl old?
  5 Are Lion Boy and Spider Boy clever?
  6 Is Cat Girl stupid?
4 1 Yes, he is.
  2 No, he isn't.
  3 Yes, she is.
  4 No, they aren't.
  5 Yes, they are.
  6 No, she isn't.
5 1 Who is he? He's Batman.
  2 Who are they? They're Oasis.
  3 Who is she? She's Cleopatra.
  4 Who are they? They're Tom and Jerry.
  5 Who is he? He's Tiger Woods.
  6 Who is she? She's Björk.

Classwork suggestion
Either bring to class or ask students to bring magazine pictures of famous people. Put students in groups of about 3–6 and give each student two or three pictures. In their groups, students think of three appropriate adjectives and make questions about the people which are either true or false. Groups take it in turns to show their pictures and ask questions about them, starting with *Who ... ?* and then questions using the adjectives. The other groups compete to give the correct answer and the teacher keeps score on the board. This activity can be used as an opportunity to monitor pronunciation by eliciting student corrections which score additional points.

Student's Book answers
6 1 I'm 2 Who 3 you 4 I'm 5 You're 6 who's
7 Answers will vary.

Classwork suggestion
To check exercise 7, get students to ask and answer the questions in open pairs round the class.

Student's Book answers
Puzzle
  1 21 (the number 3 is added to the previous number in the sequence)
  2 12 (the number 2, then 3, then 4, is added to the previous number in the box)
  3 25 (the numbers in the boxes are the squares of 2, 3, 4 and 5)

Pairwork suggestion
If your students enjoy this kind of puzzle, they can make their own set of four squares with three alternative answers and ask their partners to work out the solution.

Worksheet

Extra vocabulary: *late, ugly, weak*

A and B Use activity A for revision of adjectives before exercise 3. There are twenty-one adjectives in the word square. You could give your students a time limit and then ask how many words they have found. Elicit words and write them on the board.
Answers
→ thirsty, OK, hungry, tired, crazy, hot, late, busy, expensive, short
↓ clean, wrong, happy, young, dirty, ill, right, fast
↘ old, tall, slow

Pairwork suggestion Students use the chart in exercise 2 and other adjectives to make questions about themselves and their classmates. (*Am I tall? Are you happy?* etc.); their partners give true short answers.

Use activity B to preteach the adjectives listed. Then ask students to write the words under the pictures for written record.
Answers 1 beautiful 2 strong 3 clever 4 ugly 5 weak
  6 stupid 7 brave

Who are you?

A Find 21 adjectives.

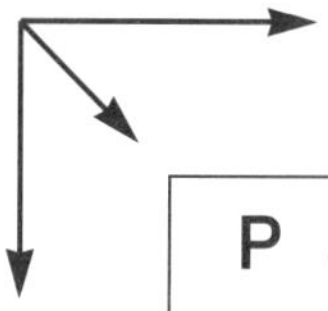

```
P J U W L A N H T K V B I T Q
T H I R S T Y R C I Z W M O T
I T R O K B S I O L E F I G L
Z H U N G R Y D N L M A V T A
O U X G V I T I R E D S N R N
Q C R A Z Y M R L C W T S E C
L C P H H O T T X F R L A T E
F L T A B U S Y Z Q I W P L K
O E X P E N S I V E G M G A L
H A I P K G P L A P H I S A N
J N E Y C T S H O R T G T P W
B L E G J O V S H W P E I G N
```

B Put the words with the pictures.

beautiful   brave   clever   strong   stupid   ugly   weak

1 It's _____beautiful_____ .

2 He's _____ .

3 They're _____ .

4 It's  _____ .   **5** She's  _____ .   **6** It's  _____ .   **7** She's _____ .

From **GRAMMAR WORKS 1** by Mick Gammidge
© Cambridge University Press 1998

PHOTOCOPIABLE

3 A star prize! What is it?

Nouns and their plural forms
Articles *a* and *an*
What + be ... ?

Nouns: Form
See Student's Book page 61 for spelling rules.

Pronunciation
The pronunciation of plural *-s* is either /s/ or /z/ depending on the last sound of the singular noun.
- Unvoiced consonant /p, t, k, f, θ/ plural *-s* is pronounced /s/.
- Vowel or voiced consonant /b, d, g, v, ŋ, m, n, l, r/, plural *-s* is pronounced /z/.
- Words ending in /s, z, ʃ, ʒ, tʃ, dʒ/, plural *-es* is pronounced /ɪz/. (Note that it is difficult to pronounce these plurals without the extra vowel.)

Articles *a* and *an*: Form
Nouns beginning with consonants take *a* as the indefinite article. Words beginning with vowels take *an* except where an initial *u* is pronounced /juː/ (e.g. *university*).

Pronunciation
A is usually pronounced /ə/ and *an* is usually pronounced /ən/. (The pronunciations /eɪ/ and /æn/ are occasionally used for emphasis.)

Vocabulary
Nouns: *alarm clock, apple, baby, bag, bike, cake, camera, child, city, clock, computer, dictionary, dish, elephant, exercise bike, exercise book, fox, glass, ice cream, ice cream maker, key, knife, man, match, mouse, orange, party, pen, people, person, prize, sheep, star, star prize, story, television, tooth, umbrella, watch, wolf, woman, zoo*
Pronoun: *what*
Verb: *win*
Adjectives: *blue, red, three*
Articles: *a, an, the*

Preview activity
Ask students to look at the competition leaflet in exercise 1. Ask them what it is. Use the leaflet to elicit or preteach *competition*, *prize* and *win*. With monolingual groups in their own country, you can bring in a competition in the students' own language from a magazine, for example. (You could ask monolingual groups in their own language if they do competitions and if they have ever won anything.)

Student's Book answers
1b 1 What is it?
  2 What are they?
 c 1 (It's) a car.
  2 (They're) a computer, an exercise bike (and) a television(.)
 d What is it?
2b dishes, babies, bags, cakes
3

s	es	ies	irregular
zoos	glasses	parties	teeth
elephants	foxes	cities	sheep

4a a camera   an exercise bike
  a television   an alarm clock

▶ Worksheet A
Pairwork suggestion
Students write a list of ten more singular nouns and test their partners who write *a* or *an* as appropriate. To check, they read out their answers to each other.

Student's Book answers
5 1 It's a glass.
  2 It's an exercise bike.
  3 It's a party.
  4 It's an alarm clock.
  5 It's an ice cream.
  6 It's a cake.

▶ Worksheet B and C
Student's Book answers
6 1 What are they? They're sheep.
  2 What are they? They're foxes.
  3 What are they? They're wolves.
  4 What is it? It's a lion.
  5 What is it? It's an elephant.
  6 What is it? It's a mouse.

Classwork suggestion
Play a space alien game. Nominate one student to be the space alien and divide the rest of the class into teams. Explain that the space alien has come to earth knowing only two questions: *What is it? What are they?* and her/his mission is to learn the names of as many things as possible. The 'alien' asks each team in turn a question about things in the room. The teacher keeps score of the teams' correct answers and monitors for pronunciation. (If it is possible, going outside the classroom gives more scope for this game. You can then put the class into smaller groups and nominate several 'aliens'.)

Student's Book answers
7 Answers will vary.

Puzzle
Possible words: bag(s), bike(s), cake(s), camera(s), mice, match(es), dish, city, cities, party, parties, sheep, watch(es)

Classwork suggestion
If your students enjoy this kind of word puzzle, then they can make their own similar puzzles in groups and exchange them with other groups. If you wish to introduce an element of competition, give a time limit for each puzzle and see which group has the most correct words at the end.

Worksheet

A Use this activity after exercise 4 for revision and practice.
  Answers 1 a camera 2 a watch 3 a bag 4 glasses
      5 a clock 6 dishes 7 a computer 8 a television
      9 an exercise bike 10 a bike

B and C Use these activities after exercise 5 for revision and practice.
  Answers B 1 fox 2 mouse 3 elephant 4 sheep 5 cat
      6 lion 7 wolf
    C 1 foxes 2 mice 3 elephants 4 sheep 5 cats
      6 lions 7 wolves

A Complete the shopping lists.

1	a camera
2	
3	
4	
5	

6	
7	
8	
9	
10	

B What are they? Write the words on the pictures.

1 fox / foxes

2

3

4

5

6

7

C Write the plural forms on the pictures in activity B.

4 It's an excellent film!

Be + article + adjective + noun constructions

Meaning
- There are many different uses of definite and indefinite articles in English and many irregularities. This unit introduces the following distinction. We use *a/an* with singular nouns that the listener is not familiar with when they are first mentioned. When the noun is mentioned again, we use *the* because we are now familiar with it. (We tend to use the pronoun to mention things the second time, except where they could be ambiguous.)
- We also use *the* for all nouns which are unique, like *the sun* and *the sky*, even when they are first mentioned.

Form
- Adjectives always come after the article and before the noun.
- The indefinite article (*a* or *an*) agrees with the first sound of the adjective, not the noun.

Pronunciation
The pronunciation of *the* is /ðə/ unless it comes immediately before a vowel sound when it is pronounced /ðiː/, e.g. /ðiː/ *actors*.

Vocabulary
Adjectives: *angry, dangerous, excellent, exciting, frightening, funny, good, great, hardworking, lazy, not bad, serious, tidy, two, unfriendly, untidy, very good*
Nouns: *actor, adventure, ant, dog, film, leopard, metre, personality, personality test, sky, sun, test, TV*

▶ **Worksheet A**

Student's Book answers
1 **** = excellent
2a 1 It's an excellent film.
   2 It's a great adventure.
 b They're great actors.
 d 1 She's **a** good actor.
   2 He's **a** funny man.
   3 It's **an** exciting adventure.
3 1 He's a tall man.
   2 It's an exciting film.
   3 He's a young boy/child.
   4 It's an expensive computer.
   5 She's a short woman.
   6 He's an old man.
4a *Batman Forever* is (1) **an** excellent film! (2) **The** film's exciting.
 b *Batman Forever* is (1) **a** great adventure. (2) **The** adventure is exciting.
5 1 The man is 2 metres.
   2 The film is great.
   3 The boy/child is 2.
   4 The computer is $100,000.
   5 The woman is 1.25 metres.
   6 The man is 99.
6 1 She isn't an untidy person. She's tidy.
   2 She isn't a sad person. She's happy.
   3 She isn't a serious person. She's funny.
   4 She isn't an unfriendly person. She's friendly.
   5 She isn't a lazy person. She's hardworking.

Pairwork extension
Elicit the question form. Students practise asking each other the questions in the questionnaire: A: *Are you an untidy person?* B: *No, I'm not. I'm a tidy person.* Follow the practice with either open-pairs demonstrations or question and answer chain round the class.

▶ **Worksheet B** and **C**

Student's Book answers
7 Answers will vary.
Puzzle
a **c**lever **c**at – the first letter of the adjective and the first letter of the noun are the same.

Classwork suggestion
Chain round the class a free association of appropriate adjective/noun combinations. Start by giving a noun, e.g. *a table*. S1 then adds an adjective: *a small table*; S2 changes the noun: *a small boy*; S3 changes the adjective: *a clever boy*; S4 changes the noun: *a clever dog*; S5: *a dangerous dog,* and so on.

Worksheet

A Preteach/Elicit the words for activity A as a preview to the unit. You can use the pictures in the activity but tell students not to write the words on their worksheets yet. Students then do the activity from memory for consolidation and written record.
  Answers Across: 1 funny 3 film 5 adventure 6 exciting
           7 TV 8 great
           Down: 1 frightening 2 excellent 4 actor

B and C Students do these activities for vocabulary practice after exercise 6 (and **Pairwork extension**).
  Answers B 1 untidy 2 unfriendly 3 lazy 4 serious
         C 1 funny 2 friendly 3 hardworking 4 lazy
             5 untidy 6 serious 7 unfriendly 8 tidy

Extension activity Students write full sentences about the pictures, e.g. *It's a funny comic.*

A Complete the crossword.
(adj = adjective; n = noun)

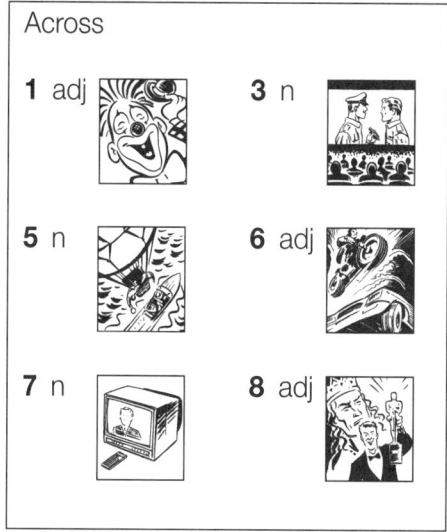
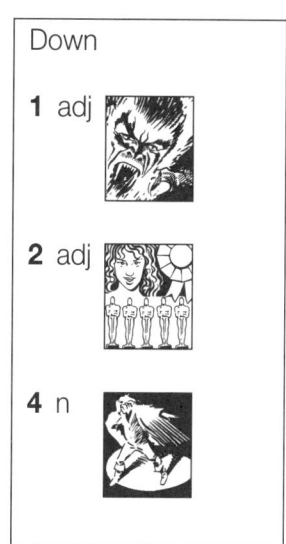

Across

1 adj

3 n

5 n

6 adj

7 n

8 adj

Down

1 adj

2 adj

4 n

B Write the opposite adjectives.

1 tidy	2
untidy	friendly

3 hardworking	4
	funny

C Match the adjectives in activity B with the pictures.

1

f u n n y

2

3

4

5

6

7

8

These are my posters

Possessive adjectives
Demonstratives

Adjectives: Form
- Possessive adjectives, like other adjectives, come before the noun.
- Possessive adjectives of nouns other than pronouns (e.g. *Paulo's*, *fox's*) have -'s endings which students may confuse with the contraction of *is*.
- Note that the possessive form of names and nouns that end in -*s* are sometimes written without the extra -*s*, just having an apostrophe (e.g. *Carlos'* or *Carlos's*).
- Possessive forms of plurals have the apostrophe after the final -*s* and no genitive -*s* is added.
- Irregular possessive adjectives are formed like singular nouns (e.g. *women* – *women's*.)

Pronunciation
The pronunciation of genitive -*s* can be /s/, /z/ or /ɪz/ following the same rules as plural -*s*.

Demonstratives: Meaning
Demonstratives have a range of subtle functions but here we focus on their usage based on an object's relative distance from the speaker.

Pronunciation
The pronunciation of *this* and *these* depends on students' ability to distinguish the vowel /ɪ/ (*this*) from /iː/ (*these*). The two vowels are not distinguished in many languages and may be a problem for students.

Vocabulary
Nouns: *bed, bedroom, boat, brother, CD, chair, chicken, cow, desk, farmer, home, horse, inventor, mother, music, name, pig, poster, singer, sister, song, telescope*
Adjectives: *only, underground, wild*
Possessive adjectives: *her, his, its, my, our, their, your*
Demonstrative pronouns: *that, these, this, those*

Student's Book answers
1b 1 B   2 C   3 A
2 he – his   they – their   it – its   she – her
Kylie – Kylie's
3 1 His name is Wallace.
2 Its name is Gromit.
3 Her name is Kylie.
4 Their names are Wallace and Gromit.
5 My name is Paulo.
6 Our names are Paulo and Carlos.
4 1 It's Hank's telescope. It's his telescope.
2 It's Dollar's chair. It's its chair.
3 It's Hank's boat. It's his boat.
4 They're Betty's CDs. They're her CDs.
5 It's Hank's desk. It's his desk.
6 It's Dollar's bed. It's its bed.

▶ Worksheet A
5

	near	far	1	2+
this	✓	✗	✓	✗
these	✓	✗	✗	✓
that	✗	✓	✓	✗
those	✗	✓	✗	✓

6 1 This is my dog. Those are my sheep.
2 That's my dog. Those are my sheep.
3 That's my dog. These are my sheep.
4 This is my dog. These are my sheep.

Classwork suggestion
Chain *this/that/these/those* round the class. Teacher says to SI (indicating/pointing as appropriate): *This is my bag, that's your desk.*
S1 to S2: *This is my desk, those are your books.*
S 2 to S3: *These are my books, that's your chair,* and so on.
You can use this as an opportunity to review the names of objects in the room which students know. (The chain also emphasises relative distance, so even though the student being addressed may be sitting next to the speaker, when the speaker uses *this/these* to refer to themselves, they use *that/those* to refer to the addressee.)

Student's Book answers
7 Answers will vary.

▶ Worksheet B
Student's Book answers
Puzzle
Tom (Tom's mother's only brother's only sister = Tom's mother; so Tom's mother's only child = Tom.)

Worksheet

Extra vocabulary: *aunt, book, cassette, comic, daughter, drawer, father, grandfather, grandmother, husband, table, uncle, wife*

A Use this activity after exercise 4 for revision and extension.
Answers 1 poster   2 a bike   3 a television   4 a computer
5 a chair   6 drawers   7 a bed   8 a boat   9 a desk
10 an alarm clock   11 a table   12 CDs   13 cassettes
14 comics   15 books   16 a telescope

B Use this activity after exercise 7 to present the names of family members.
Answers 1 son   2 daughter   3 mother   4 father   5 brother
6 sister   7 grandmother   8 grandfather   9 husband
10 wife   11 aunt   12 uncle

Extension activity Students use the family tree in pairs to test each other. One student can write and/or say the first part of the sentence. The second student finishes it.

Pairwork suggestion Students draw diagrams representing their family trees but they do not write the names of their relatives on the diagram. They then give the diagrams to their partners who have to ask questions and complete the family trees, e.g. *What's your father's name? His name is … What are your father's parents' names? Their names are …* , and so on. When students have completed the task, they can show their completed family trees to their partner to check their answers.

A Look at the picture of the bedroom. Write the names of the things.

1 _____
2 _____
3 _____
4 _____
5 _____
6 _____ drawers _____
7 _____
8 _____

9 _____
10 _____
11 _____ a table _____
12 _____
13 _____ cassettes _____
14 _____
15 _____
16 _____

B Look at the family tree. Complete the sentences.

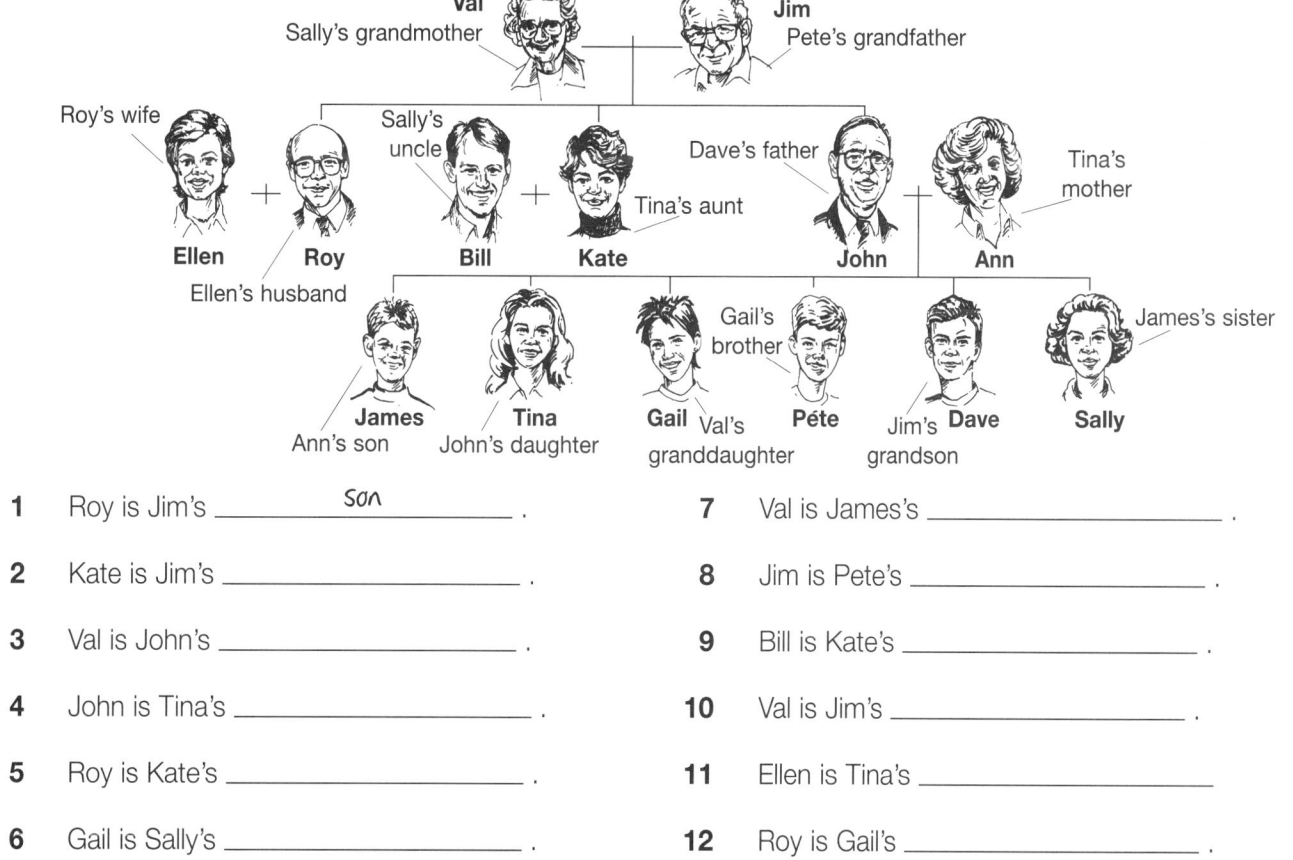

Val — Sally's grandmother
Jim — Pete's grandfather
Roy's wife — Ellen
Ellen's husband — Roy
Sally's uncle — Bill
Tina's aunt — Kate
Dave's father — John
Tina's mother — Ann
James — Ann's son
Tina — John's daughter
Gail — Val's granddaughter
Gail's brother — Péte
Dave — Jim's grandson
Sally — James's sister

1 Roy is Jim's _____ son _____ .

2 Kate is Jim's _____ .

3 Val is John's _____ .

4 John is Tina's _____ .

5 Roy is Kate's _____ .

6 Gail is Sally's _____ .

7 Val is James's _____ .

8 Jim is Pete's _____ .

9 Bill is Kate's _____ .

10 Val is Jim's _____ .

11 Ellen is Tina's _____ .

12 Roy is Gail's _____ .

From **GRAMMAR WORKS 1** by Mick Gammidge
© Cambridge University Press 1998

6 Whose breakfast is this?

Possessive pronouns
Whose + noun + be + pronoun?

Pronouns: Form
- Possessive pronouns may cause confusion because some have the same form as their possessive adjectives, e.g. *his coat/his*, while others are different, e.g. *her coat/hers*.
- *Its* is not used as a possessive pronoun, only as a possessive adjective.

Whose: Form
The word order in *Whose* questions is quite flexible: *Whose X is this/it?*; *Whose is this/it?*; *Whose is this X?* Only the first two structures are presented here.

Pronunciation
The pronunciation of *whose* may confuse students because it is the same as *who's*.

Vocabulary
Nouns: *bacon, ball, beans, book, breakfast, burger, car, chips, dad, egg, fish, fishing rod, glove, mum, scarf, shirt, shoe, skates, sock, teddy, toast, video*
Possessive pronouns: *hers, his, mine, ours, theirs, yours*
Pronoun: *whose*

▶ **Worksheet A**
Student's Book answers
1b 1 Babs 2 Clare 3 Al 4 Dave
2
It's my breakfast.	It's **mine**.
It's your breakfast.	It's **yours**.
It's his breakfast.	It's **his**.
It's her breakfast.	It's **hers**.
It's our breakfast.	It's **ours**.
It's their breakfast.	It's **theirs**.
It's Dave's breakfast.	It's **Dave's**.
It's the dog's breakfast.	It's **the dog's**.
It's the dogs' breakfast.	It's **the dogs'**.

3 1 mine 2 ours 3 theirs 4 yours 5 hers 6 his
4a 1 Whose breakfast is this?
    2 Is this yours?
 b 1 Whose breakfasts are those?
    2 Are those yours?
5 1 Whose shirt is this?
    2 Whose socks are these?
    3 Is this yours?
    4 Are these yours?
    5 Whose shoe is this?

Classwork suggestion
Chain round the class. S1 says: *This is my X. It is mine.* S2 says to S1: *That is your X. It is yours.* S3 says to S4: *That is her/his X. It is hers/his.* S4 turns to S5 and says: *This is my Y. It is mine*, and the chain continues. After a first chain, you could divide the class into rows and repeat the activity as a race between the rows.

Classwork suggestion
Each student secretly puts an object which belongs to them into a bag. When all the objects are in the bag, pull out one and ask *Is this yours, X?* You have three chances to guess the right owner after which the question *Whose ... is this?* is asked. The owner goes next, picking another object out of the bag and again has three chances to guess the right owner. When all the objects have been identified, students write down sentences for each object, e.g. *The pen is Niko's.* The aim is to see how many correct owners of objects students can remember.

▶ **Worksheet B**
Student's Book answers
6 1 is mine 2 are hers 3 is theirs 4 is his
7 Answers will vary.
Puzzle
A = fish B = bike C = bag D = shoe

Worksheet

Extra vocabulary: *cereal, dress, fruit, hat, jeans, skirt, trousers*

A Preteach/Elicit the words for activity A as a preview to the unit. You can use the pictures in the activity but tell students not to write the words on their worksheets yet. Students then do the activity from memory for consolidation and written record.
Answers 1 fruit 2 burgers 3 chips 4 bacon 5 eggs
            6 toast 7 beans 8 cereal

B You can use the pictures in activity B to preteach the clothes words listed before exercise 6. Point out to students that *jeans* and *trousers* (and other clothes with two legs) are always plural forms. Then ask students to write the words in the list for written record.
Answers 1 socks 2 skirt 3 shoes 4 jeans 5 hat
            6 trousers 7 dress 8 scarf 9 shirt 10 gloves

A Write the words with the pictures.

bacon   beans   burgers   cereal   chips   eggs   fruit   toast

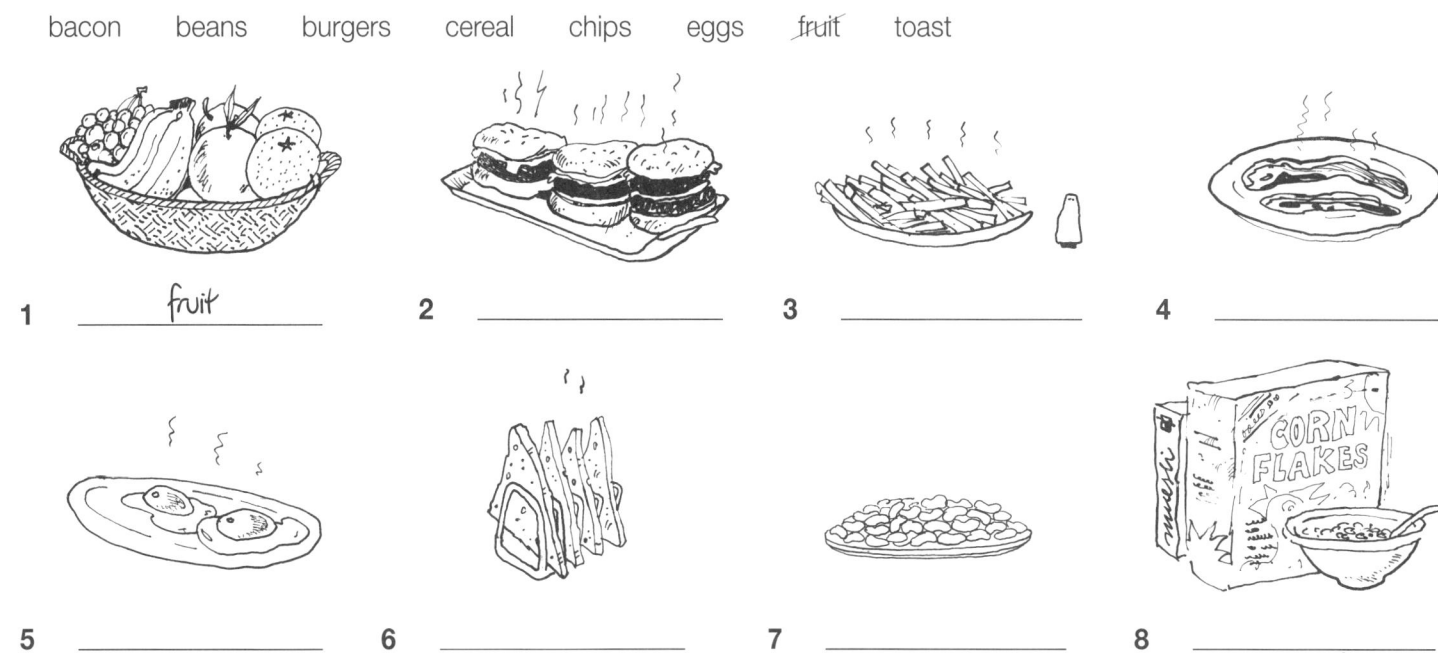

1   fruit

2 _____

3 _____

4 _____

5 _____

6 _____

7 _____

8 _____

B Complete the woman's list.

1   Socks

2 _____

3 _____

4 _____

5 _____

6 _____

7 _____

8 _____

9 _____

10 _____

1
1 It's old and it's dirty. What is it?
2 They're fast and they're dangerous. What are they?
3 It's strong and it's slow. What is it?
4 He's short and he's happy. Who is he?
5 She's tall and she's sad. Who is she?

2
1 It's a car.
2 They're leopards.
3 It's an elephant.
4 He's Bill.
5 She's Ann.

3
1 Are they young?   Yes, they are.
2 Are they friendly?   Yes, they are.
3 Are they beautiful?   Yes, they are.
4 Are they clever?   No, they aren't!
5 Is it new?   No, it isn't.
6 Is it red?   No, it isn't.
7 Is it fast?   Yes, it is.
8 Is it expensive?   Er, yes, it is!

4a
1 It's an expensive bike.
2 It's a funny comic.
3 It's an old university.
4 He's an untidy boy.
5 It's an exciting film.
6 It's a lazy cat.

b
1 The bike is expensive.
2 The comic is funny.
3 The university is old.
4 The boy is untidy.
5 The film is exciting.
6 The cat is lazy.

5

I	my	mine
you	your	yours
he	his	his
she	her	hers
it	its	~~its~~
Sue	Sue's	Sue's
the cat	the cat's	the cat's
we	our	ours
you	your	yours
they	their	theirs
the cats	the cats'	the cats'

6
1 Whose mouse is this?
   That's mine.
2 Whose burger/sandwich is this?
   That's hers.
3 Whose socks are these?
   Those are his.

1

a/an	singular	plural
an	apple	apples
a	glass	glasses
a	knife	knives
a	baby	babies
an	umbrella	umbrellas

2
1 He's a tall boy.
2 She's an old woman.
3 It's a dirty car.
4 They're happy children.
5 He's a strong man.

3
1 What is it?   It's an alarm clock.
   Whose alarm clock is it?   It's Jack's.
2 What is it?   It's a camera.
   Whose camera is it?   It's Alex's.
3 What is it?   It's an exercise bike.
   Whose exercise bike is it?   It's Sue's.
4 What are they?   They're dictionaries.
   Whose dictionaries are they?   They're Chris's.

4
1 These are her skates.
2 Those are her CDs.
3 That's her teddy.
4 That's her bed.
5 Those are her socks.
6 This is her chair.
7 This is her desk.
8 These are her shoes.

1 Write *a/an* and the singular and plural forms.

a/an	singular		plural
an	apple		_____
____	_____		_____
____	_____		_____
____	_____		_____
____	_____		_____

2 Write sentences about the pictures. Use an adjective for each sentence.

1 He's a tall boy. _____

2 _____

3 _____

4 _____

5 _____

3 Write questions about the pictures with *what* and *whose*. Then write the answers.

1 What is it?

   It's an alarm clock.

   Whose alarm clock is it?

   It's Jack's.

2 _____

   _____

   _____

   _____

3 _____

   _____

   _____

   _____

4 _____

   _____

   _____

   _____

4 Write the mother's sentences about the bedroom. Use *this/that/these/those*.

This is my daughter's bedroom!

1 These are her skates. _____

2 _____

3 _____

4 _____

5 _____

6 _____

7 _____

8 _____

7 Tina hasn't got a home

Have got affirmative, negative and question forms

Meaning
Although grammatically a present perfect, *have got* has a present simple function and is used far more than present simple *have* to show possession, attachment, etc. in the present.

Form
- This is the first time students have encountered auxiliary verbs. The important points for students to grasp are firstly that the auxiliary verb *have/has* changes to agree with the subject and secondly, that only the auxiliary, not the main verb *got*, changes place with the subject to form questions.
- Students may confuse *has* and *is* in the contracted forms as they are spelt and pronounced the same.

Pronunciation
Contractions are generally used in spoken English and full forms are generally used in written English. The pronunciation of the contraction -*'s* is /s/, /z/ or /ɪz/, following the same rules as plural -*s*. Full forms are not stressed except for emphasis and their weak forms are /həv/, /əv/, /həz/ and /əz/, compared to /hæv/ and /hæz/ when stressed.

Vocabulary
Nouns: *daughter, finger, flat, garden, grandparents, headache, house, leg, mouth, nose, pet, school, stomach-ache, sweet, toothache, wife, work*
Adjectives: *bad, broken, sore*
Verbs: *have got (has got)*

Preview activity
Preteach the word *pet* (you could draw a person with a cat and dog, elicit the names of the animals and give *pet* as the general term for animals which live in the home). Ask students what other animals are pets.

Student's Book answers
1b 1 Yes, she is. 2 No, they aren't.

2a
I   you •   • has
we they •   • hasn't
                    • have
she he it •   • haven't

b ? Has she got a home?
+ She has got a home.
− She hasn't got a home.

c
Have you got a dog? •   • Yes, I have
Has he got a dog? •   • Yes, he has.
                             • No, he hasn't.
                             • No, I haven't.

Class/Pairwork suggestion
Set up a substitution drill. Write +, − and ? symbols on the board and give a noun, e.g. *elephant.* Then give the pronoun, e.g. *she,* and point to one of the symbols, e.g. (−). Class or S1 says *She hasn't got an elephant.* Point to another symbol (?) and class/S1 says *Has she got an elephant?* Keep pointing to the different symbols, changing either the pronoun or the noun. When students have got the idea, one student can drill the rest of the class at the board or students can drill each other in pairs.

▶ *Worksheet A*

Student's Book answers
3 1 Joe has got a flat.   2 Joe hasn't got a garden.
3 Joe has got a cat.   4 Mr and Mrs Mill have got a house.
5 Mr and Mrs Mill have got a daughter.
6 Mr and Mrs Mill have got a mouse.

4 1 I've got a toothache.   2 You've got a bad tooth.
3 He's got a sore finger.   4 They've got broken legs.
5 I've got a headache.   6 She's got a stomach-ache.

▶ *Worksheet B*

Student's Book answers
5 1 Has your school got a computer?
2 Have you got a computer (at home)?
3 Has your father got a computer (at work)?
4 Has your mother got a computer (at work)?
5 Have your grandparents got a computer?

6 Answers will vary.

Project work suggestion
Students collate the answers for the class (perhaps assign one question to each student so they can ask everyone in the class). Students draw bar graphs to show results as in exercise 6, but with numbers instead of percentages. Students then write sentences about the graph, e.g. *Eight fathers have got a computer at work.*

Student's Book answers
7 Answers will vary.

Pairwork suggestion
Students practise asking and answering questions which they form from the nouns given in exercise 7, e.g. *Have you got a watch?*, *Has your father got a telescope?*

Classwork extension
Play 'Find someone who …'. Put a list of singular nouns/possessions on the board, including some which are unusual but which someone in the class will probably have. Students then go round the class asking each other *Have you got … ?* until they have found a person for every item. (Note that students don't encounter *some* and *any* until the next unit so the nouns must be singular.)

Student's Book answers
Puzzle Anne = 2, Bill = 3, Clare = 1; altogether = 6

Worksheet

Extra vocabulary: *arm, door, ear, eye, face, foot, hair, hand, head, lift, stairs, stomach, window*

A Use activity A to introduce the vocabulary needed for exercise 3. Students should be able to find the correct words by eliminating all the words they know so far. Consequently, this activity could take the form of a race between groups.
Answers 1 door 2 flats 3 garden 4 house 5 lift 6 pet
7 stairs   8 window

B Elicit/Preteach the body parts after exercise 4. Students complete the words for consolidation and written record. For further practice, students can write the vocabulary, with any other body parts you wish to add, on sticky labels and label each other.
Answers 1 hair 2 face 3 ear 4 eye 5 head 6 nose
7 mouth 8 teeth 9 arm 10 stomach 11 hand
12 finger 13 leg 14 foot

A Choose the correct word for the things in the picture.

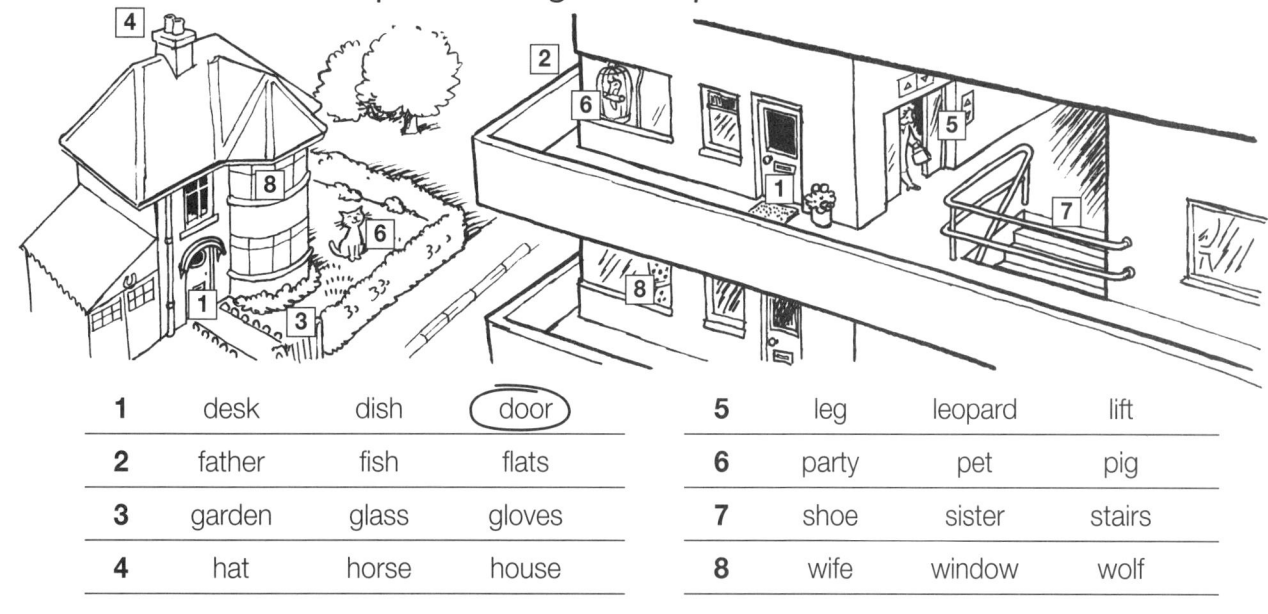

1	desk	dish	(door)
2	father	fish	flats
3	garden	glass	gloves
4	hat	horse	house

5	leg	leopard	lift
6	party	pet	pig
7	shoe	sister	stairs
8	wife	window	wolf

B Look at the picture and complete the words below.

finger arm nose hand stomach head eye teeth ~~hair~~ face leg mouth ear foot

1	h	a	i	r
2	f			
3	e			
4	e			
5	h			
6	n			
7	m			
8	t			
9	a			
10	s			
11	h			
12	f			
13	l			
14	f			

There is / There are affirmative, negative and question forms
Some, any

There is / There are: Meaning
* *There is / There are* is used to talk about the existence of things. (In this general usage, *there* does not necessarily indicate any distance/location of the thing in relation to the speaker.)

Form
* Although *there* comes before the verb, like a subject, the verb must agree with the following noun. Example: *There **is a man**. There **are two men***.
* *There + is* contracts to *there's* (except in formal written English). There is no similar written contraction for *there are*, **there're*.

Pronunciation
The pronunciation of *there* is generally /ðeə/ and is unstressed. As the verb *be* is also generally unstressed in this structure, *there are* is pronounced /ðeər ə/.

Some, any: Form
Some and *any* are used with plural nouns. In this structure, *some* is used in plural, affirmative sentences (see also uncountables: Unit 9) and *any* is used in plural negatives and generally in question forms (though *some* may be used in questions where the speaker expects the answer 'yes'). In all singular forms, *a/an* is used.

Vocabulary
Nouns: *axe, box, car park, cassette, column, comic, cupboard, lift, magazine, radio, restaurant, row, shop, square, swimming pool, telephone*
Adjectives: *black, white*

▶ *Worksheet* A and B

Student's Book answers
1b a ✓ b ✗ c ✗
2

	+	−	?
singular (1)	a/an	a/an	a/an
plural (2+)	some	any	any

3

There	a bag, **an** orange, **some** comics, **any** CDs.
there	a bag, **an** apple, **any** watches?
there	is, are, isn't, aren't.

Groupwork suggestion
Bring different common objects to class (which students know the names of in English), and place them on a table at the front of the class. Allow students to look at the objects for a given time (e.g. one minute) and then cover them with a cloth or newspaper. In their groups, students write sentences using *There is / There are*. Groups get points for remembering the individual objects and for correct grammar.

Student's Book answers
4 1 There is a box.   2 There isn't a ball.
    3 There isn't a bike.   4 There aren't any books.
    5 There is an axe.   6 There are some cassettes.
    7 There are some magazines.   8 There aren't any skates.
5 1 There is a swimming pool.   2 There are some telephones.
    3 There is a car park.   4 There are some shops.
    5 There is a restaurant.   6 There is a garden.
    7 There are some lifts.
6a 1 Is there a swimming pool?   2 Are there any telephones?
    3 Is there a car park?   4 Are there any shops?
    5 Is there a restaurant?   6 Is there a garden?
    7 Are there any lifts?
  b 1 No, there isn't. 2 Yes, there are. 3 Yes, there is.
    4 No, there aren't. 5 Yes, there is. 6 No, there isn't.
    7 Yes, there are.

▶ *Worksheet* C
7 Answers will vary.

Pairwork suggestion
Students practise asking and answering questions about the contents of their bedrooms, based on the sentences they wrote in exercise 7, e.g. *Are there any posters in your bedroom? Yes, there are. / No, there aren't*. Follow the practice with either open-pairs demonstrations or chain round the class.

Student's Book answers
Puzzle
The black squares are A2, C2, B4 and C4.

Class/Pairwork suggestion
Set up a substitution drill. Write +, − and ? symbols on the board. Give a noun, e.g. *mouse*, then point to one of the symbols (?). Class or S1 asks *Is there a mouse?* Point to either a different symbol or make the noun plural or change the noun (e.g. to give student/class responses like: *There isn't a mouse. / Are there any mice?*). Again, when students have got the idea, one student can drill the class at the board or students can drill each other in pairs.

Worksheet

Extra vocabulary: *newspaper, pencil, rubber, ruler*

A and B Preteach the new words for activity A (*magazine, newspaper, pencil, radio, rubber, ruler*) as a preview to the unit. (You could use realia or simple drawings on the board.) Students do the activities, which involve a memory test and establish the context for exercise 1 in the Student's Book.

Answers a orange b key c radio d bag e ruler f cassette
        g CD h pen i magazine j apple k book l pencil
        m dictionary n newspaper o comic p rubber
        q watch r clock

C Students do activity C after exercise 6.

Answers   car park   lifts   shop

        restaurant   garden

        swimming pool   telephones

Are there any comics?

A *Write the correct letters with the words.*

- [ ] apple
- [ ] bag
- [ ] book
- [ ] cassette
- [ ] CD
- [ ] clock
- [ ] comic
- [ ] dictionary
- [ ] key
- [ ] magazine
- [ ] newspaper
- [a] orange
- [ ] pen
- [ ] pencil
- [ ] radio
- [ ] rubber
- [ ] ruler
- [ ] watch

a
b
c
d
e
f
g
h
i
j
k
l
m
n
o
p
q
r
DICTIONARY

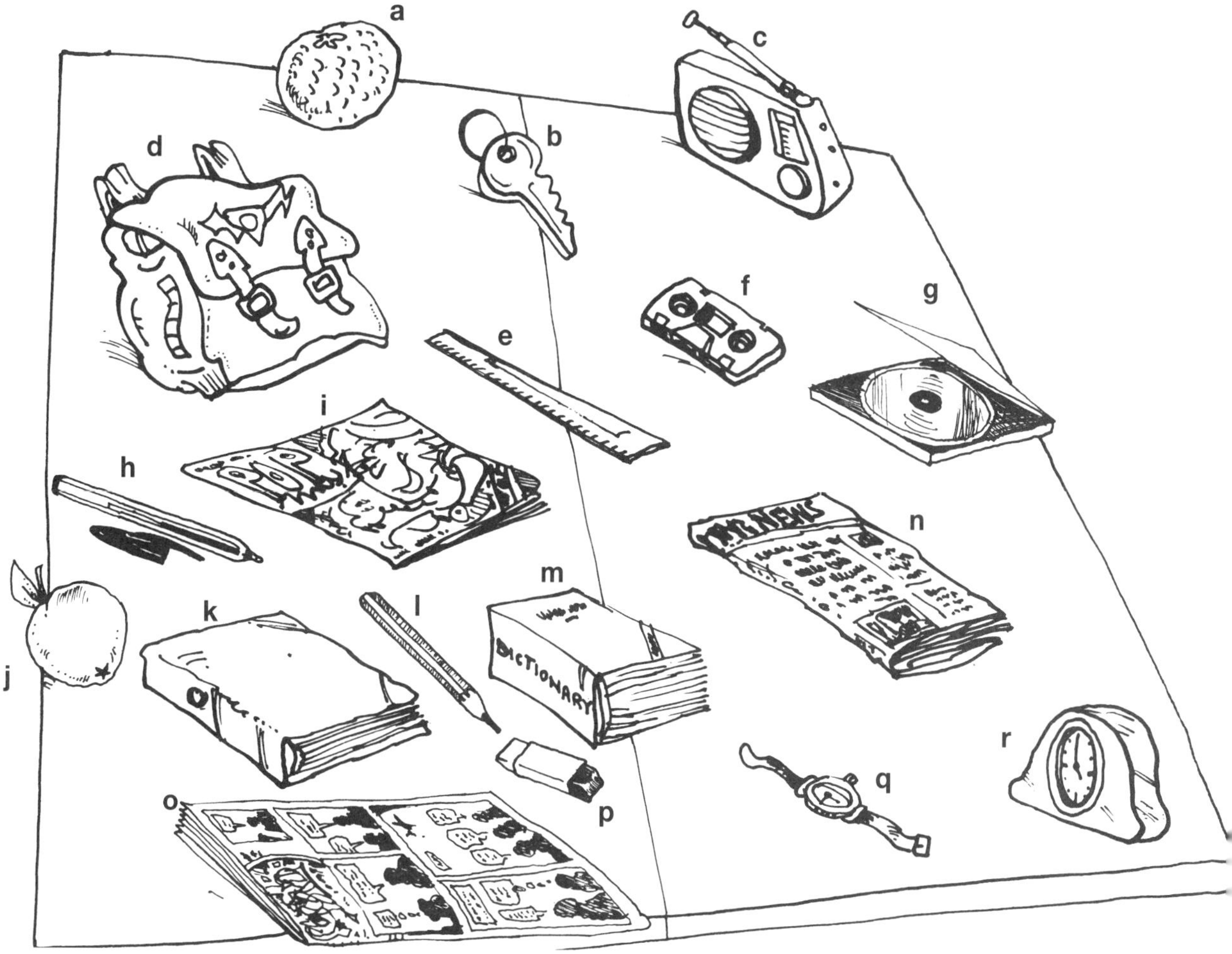

B *Look at the picture in activity A for one minute. Then close your books and write a list of the things in the picture.*

C *Draw arrows (→) from the signs to the things on the plan of the hotel.*

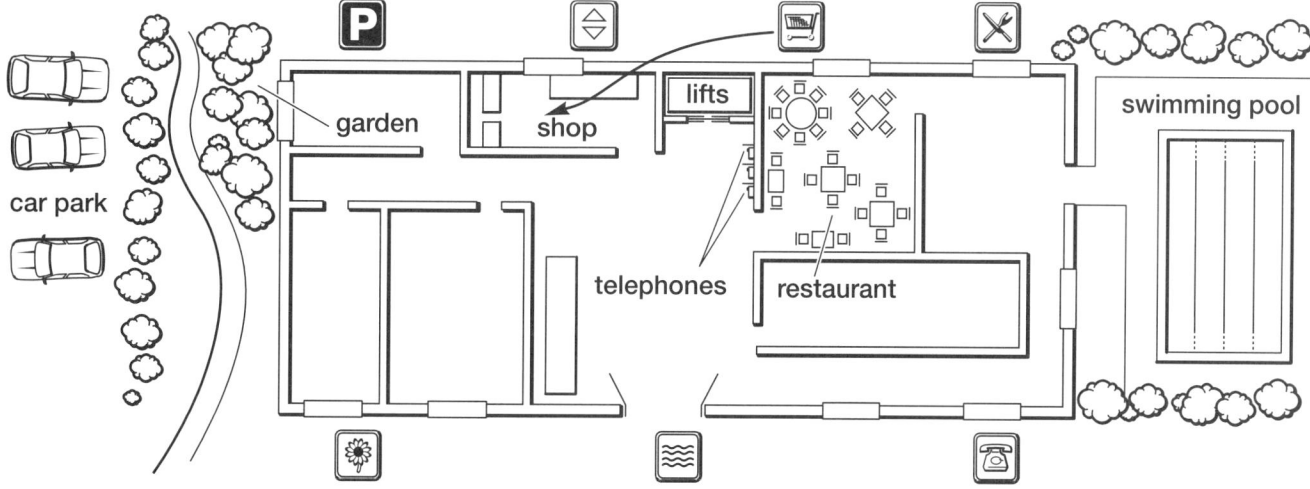

P
lifts
garden
shop
swimming pool
car park
telephones
restaurant

9 How much orange juice is there?

How much / How many
Much / Many: countable and uncountable nouns

How much / How many: Meaning
- *How many* is used for questions about quantities of countable nouns.
- *How much* is used for questions about quantities of uncountable nouns.

Countable/Uncountable: Meaning
- Countable nouns are those things we can count.
- Uncountable nouns are those nouns for which we don't usually give the number of individual items, such as liquids or solids such as salt, sugar, etc. which are quantified in terms of weights or volumes. (The distinction does not always appear clear, for example, *crisps* are countable but it is unusual to talk about specific numbers of crisps; we usually talk about *bags of crisps*.)

Form
- Uncountable nouns act as singular nouns and take third person singular forms of verbs.
- The noun can be elided where appropriate: *How much (water) is there? How many (pens) are there?*

Vocabulary
Nouns: *banana, biscuit, bottle, coffee, crisps, gram, juice, lemonade, litre, meat, oil, orange juice, sandwich, sausage, shampoo, soap, sugar, tea, toothpaste, water*
Determiner: *each*
how much ...? / how many ...?

Student's Book answers
1 a 50 grams   b 1 litre   c 34   d 3
2a 1 are   2 many, are   3 is   4 much, is
 b much – sugar, orange juice
    many – oranges, glasses

3

Countable nouns		Uncountable nouns	
bananas	eggs	cereal	meat
burgers	sandwiches	coffee	oil
cakes	sausages	lemonade	water

Groupwork suggestion
Students come up with a list of, for instance, 20 countable and uncountable nouns. The lists are then swapped with other groups who have to put *a, an, some* as appropriate in front of the nouns. The first group to complete their list with all the answers correct is the winner.

Student's Book answers
4 1 There are some biscuits.   2 There is some chicken.
 3 There is some coffee.   4 There are some sausages.
 5 There are some sandwiches. 6 There are some bananas.
 7 There is some meat.   8 There is some lemonade.
5 1 How many biscuits are there?
 2 How much chicken is there?
 3 How much coffee is there?
 4 How many sausages are there?
 5 How many sandwiches are there?
 6 How many bananas are there?
 7 How much meat is there?
 8 How much lemonade is there?

▶ Worksheet A

Groupwork suggestion
Bring in pictures from magazines with food (or other known countable or uncountable nouns). Recipe pages in glossy magazines usually have good photos of ingredients; alternatively paste up a selection of photos from magazines. Students form small groups and then pair up with another group. Give each group in each pair a picture which they can look at for a given time (say one minute). They then swap pictures and take it in turns to ask and answer questions for a given amount of time (say five minutes), e.g. *Is there any orange juice? How much juice is there?* Groups keep each other's scores and the winning group is the one with the most correct answers at the end of the time period. (You can tell students that it is to their advantage to make their questions as difficult as possible.)

Student's Book answers
6 1 any 2 there 3 much 4 some 5 many 6 are 7 are
  8 is 9 isn't

▶ Worksheet B

7 Answers will vary.

Pairwork suggestion
Students practise asking and answering questions about the things in their bathrooms based on the sentences they wrote in exercise 7, e.g. *Is there any shampoo in your bathroom?* Follow the practice with either open-pairs demonstrations or question and answer chain round the class.

Student's Book answers
Puzzle
Five: there are only two brothers altogether.

Worksheet

Extra vocabulary: *comb, hairbrush, mirror, toothbrush, towel*

A Students do this activity after exercise 5.
  Answers 1 lemonade 2 sandwiches 3 crisps 4 apples
     5 bananas 6 orange juice 7 coffee 8 cakes
     9 biscuits 10 chicken

  Extension activity Working on their own, students select three food/drink items in the picture and cross them out. (Tell them to imagine that they have been sold!) Then, in pairs and without looking at each other's worksheet, students take turns to ask questions (*Is there any … / Are there any … ?*) to find out which are their partner's missing items. The first student to find all three is the winner.

B You can use the pictures in this activity to preteach the words for the numbered illustrations before exercise 7. Then ask students to do the crossword for written record.
  Answers Down: 1 towel 2 toothpaste 3 hairbrush
     5 comb 6 soap
     Across: 2 toothbrush 4 mirror 7 shampoo

A Write the words for the food and drink in the picture.

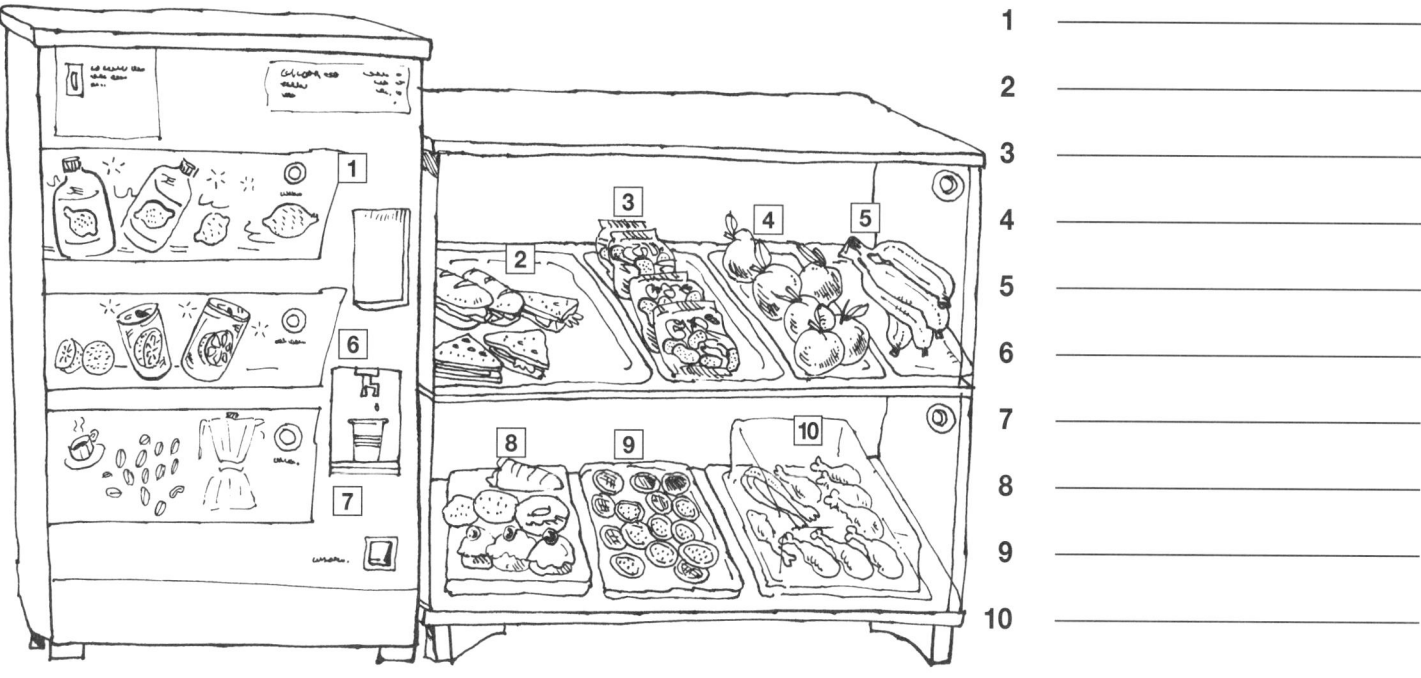

1 _____
2 _____
3 _____
4 _____
5 _____
6 _____
7 _____
8 _____
9 _____
10 _____

B Complete the crossword with the names of the things in the bathroom.

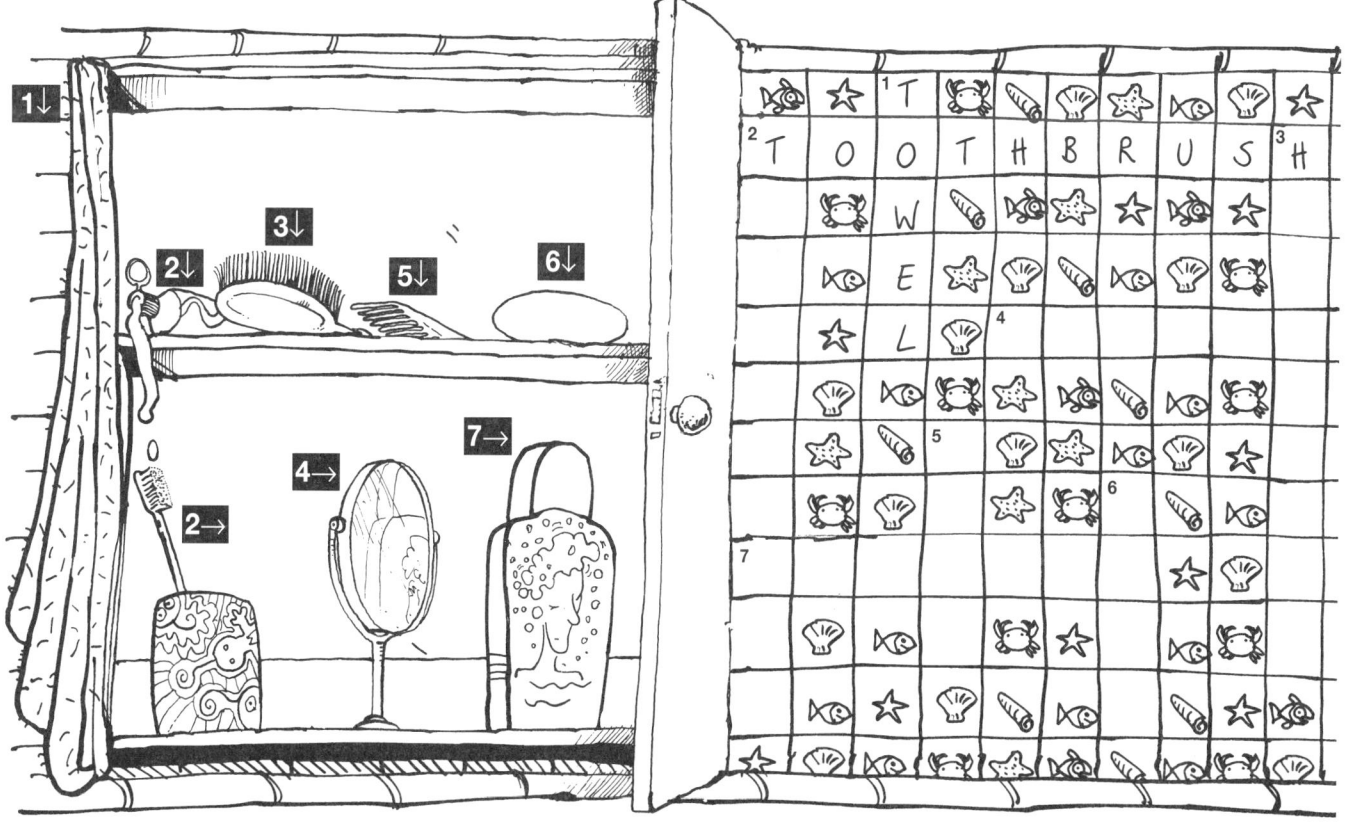

10 What's in your fridge?

Prepositions of place
Where ... ?

Prepositions: Meaning
Prepositions have a reputation for being very difficult. Here, however, we deal only with prepositions of place, which are quite straightforward in meaning and regular in usage.

Form
Prepositions of place precede the noun phrase.

Pronunciation
- Prepositions of place are not stressed (except for emphasis or contrast, which is extremely rare), and /ə/ is used in *next to*, /tə/, and *in front of* /əv/.
- The *-r* in *where*, although usually silent, is followed here by a vowel sound (*where is / where are*) and consequently pronounced.

Vocabulary
Nouns: *bank, bin, bookshop, bridge, bus stop, café, cooker, duck, fridge, jug, kitchen, newsagent, park, plate, post box, post office, river, spoon*
Prepositions: *above, behind, beside, between, by, in, in front of, next to, on, under*

▶ **Worksheet A**

Student's Book answers
1b 1 It's in the sink.
2 It's under the table.
3 They're on the table.

2

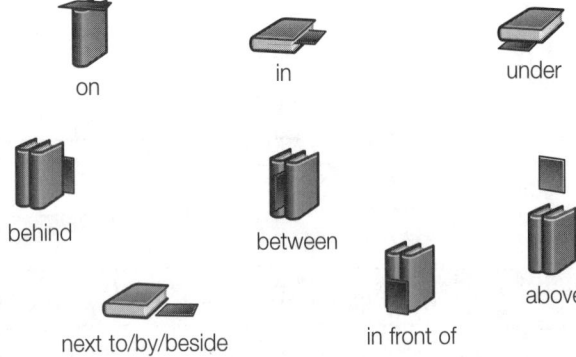

on   in   under

behind   between   above

next to/by/beside   in front of

Practice activity
Using a pen and a book, you can demonstrate the prepositions of place introduced in this unit by putting the pen in the appropriate locations relative to the book and yourself and having students repeat. Gradually get students to produce the prepositions from memory as the pen is moved.

Student's Book answers
3 1 Where is the dog?
2 Where is the newspaper?
3 Where are the keys?
4 Where is the clock?
5 Where are the books?

▶ **Worksheet B**

Student's Book answers
4 1 next to
2 on
3 in
4 between
5 in front of

Pairwork suggestion
Students draw their own picture of a scene (without letting their partner see it) and then describe it to their partner who has to draw it. They then compare the two versions.

Student's Book answers
5 1 There is a fish next to some lemonade.
2 There is some lemonade between a fish and some orange juice.
3 There is some meat above some sausages.
4 There is some chicken behind some eggs.
5 There are some eggs in front of some chicken.
6 There are some sausages under some meat.
6 1 The fish is between the lemonade and the orange juice.
2 The lemonade is next to the fish.
3 The meat is under the sausages.
4 The chicken is behind the ice cream.
5 The eggs are above the chicken.
6 The sausages are next to the eggs.

Classwork suggestion
Draw a big fridge or cupboard with shelves on the board. One student is given the pen and draws in the fridge/cupboard the food items in the respective positions that the other students suggest.

Student's Book answers
7 Answers will vary.
Puzzle
There are three ducks. Two ducks are in front of the last duck; two ducks are behind the first duck and the second duck is between the first and the last duck.

Worksheet

Extra vocabulary: *cup, floor, fork, sink, supermarket*

A You can use the pictures in activity A to preteach the items shown as a preview to the unit. Then ask students to write the words for the pictures for written record.

Answers a cooker   b fridge   c sink   d bin   e floor   f chair   g plate   h cup   i glass   j spoon   k knife   l fork   m jug   n dish   o table

B You can use the pictures in this activity to preteach the items shown before exercise 4. Then ask students to write the words on the pictures for written record.

Answers 1 bridge   2 supermarket   3 telephone   4 bus stop   5 park   6 café   7 bookshop   8 bank   9 post office   10 newsagent

A Write the correct letters with the words.

- [ ] bin
- [ ] chair
- [ ] cooker
- [ ] cup
- [ ] dish
- [ ] floor
- [ ] fork
- [ ] fridge
- [ ] glass
- [ ] jug
- [ ] knife
- [ ] plate
- [ ] sink
- [ ] spoon
- [ ] table

B Write the names of the places and things on the signs.

bank   bookshop   ~~bridge~~   bus stop   café   newsagent   park   post office   supermarket   telephone

11 Don't sit in the sun

Imperatives   affirmative and negative forms

Meaning
Imperatives are used for commands, instructions (and similar, e.g. directions), advice and informal requests.

Form
- Students are introduced to *do* in the formation of negatives. *Do* is not used in the affirmative (except for extreme emphasis).
- The contraction *don't* is usually used, except in formal written English or for emphasis, when the full form *do not* may be used.
- There is no subject in the imperative construction.

Vocabulary
Nouns: *carrot, carrot juice, classroom, computer games, drink, fruit, fruit juice, grass, hat, holiday, homework, ice, lemon, litter, midday, pattern, photo, pineapple, pineapple juice, school uniform, sunglasses, sun cream, teacher*
Verbs: *add, do, drink, drop, eat, listen, make, move, play, pour, put, run, sit, squeeze, stand, stir, take, turn, use, walk, wash, wear*
Sequencers: *finally, first, next, then*
Adjectives: *Caribbean, cool*
Adverbs: *left, right*
Preposition: *into*

▶ Worksheet A
Student's Book answers
1b 1 ✓ 2 ✗ 3 ✓ 4 ✗ 5 ✓
  c don't
2 1 **Drink** lemonade.
  2 **Don't** stand in the sun at midday.
3 1 d 2 c 3 a 4 e 5 b
4 1 Don't take photos.
  2 Turn left.
  3 Don't drop litter.
  4 Wash your hands.
  5 Don't walk on the grass.
  6 Don't turn right.
  7 Don't drink the water.

Classwork suggestion
Play 'Simple Simon Says'. Give the class instructions, e.g. *Stand up; Drink; Put your hands on your head* but preface the one you want the students to do with *Simple Simon Says (put your hands on your head)*. Students must obey Simple Simon but mustn't do the action if it is not prefaced by *Simple Simon Says* and should keep still. If students mistakenly obey unprefaced commands, they are out of the game. When they have got the idea, nominate a student to give the commands.

Groupwork suggestion
Play 'Blind Man's Derby'. Put the class into about four groups and send one member of each group out of the classroom. Arrange the chairs or desks into four lines with spaces in between like a slalom track. Blindfold the selected students and bring them back into the class. Their team mates must shout instructions/directions to enable them to get through the course – they must go round each obstacle without touching it and without missing it out. In the event of them doing either, they must go back to the beginning. The winning team is the one who safely leads their representative through the course first.

▶ Worksheet B
Student's Book answers
5 Dos: 1 Do 2 Wear 3 Listen 4 Be
  Don'ts: 1 Don't eat 2 Don't play 3 Don't sit 4 Don't run
6 1 Wash your hands.
  2 Don't stand on the/your chairs.
  3 Use a ruler.
  4 Put litter in the bin.
  5 Don't run.
7 Answers will vary.

Groupwork suggestion
Like the 'Happy Holidays' text or the school rules, students think of other areas where dos and don'ts apply, e.g. driving a car. They produce information leaflets with at least three dos and three don'ts with illustrations. Encourage humour.

Student's Book answers
Puzzle

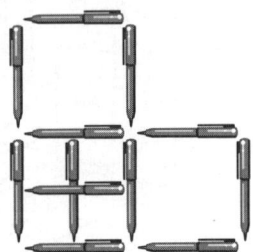

Worksheet

A Preteach the verbs as a preview to the unit; mime is a good idea. Then use the verbs to give students instructions for them to act out, e.g. *Wash your face*. (This is a good opportunity to revise prepositions of place, e.g. *Sit on your desk*.)

Students then take it in turns to give instructions to a partner. After that they do activity A for consolidation and written record.
Answers 1 drink 2 wash 3 sit 4 eat 5 listen 6 walk
         7 drop 8 turn 9 run 10 stand 11 play

B Students do this activity before exercise 5.
Answers add – 6, 8   pour – 2, 9   use – 3, 10   stir – 4, 11
         put – 5, 12   squeeze – 1, 7

A Look at the pictures. Choose the correct word for the actions.

~~drink~~ drop eat listen play run sit stand turn walk wash

1 _____ drink _____

2 _____

3 _____

4 _____

5 _____

  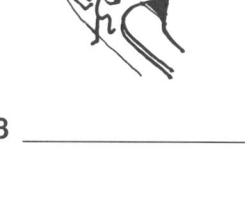  

6 _____

7 _____

8 _____

9 _____

10 _____

11 _____

B Choose two pictures for each word.

add ☐ ☐

pour ☐ ☐

use ☐ ☐

stir ☐ ☐

put ☐ ☐

squeeze [1] ☐

2 +2 = 4

From **GRAMMAR WORKS 1** by Mick Gammidge
© Cambridge University Press 1998

12 *What can you do?*

Can affirmative, negative and question forms

Meaning
Can has several functions: here it is used only for ability in the present.

Form
- *Can*, like other modal verbs, does not take third person *-s*. Nor does the main verb which follows. The main verb is always the bare infinitive (i.e. without *to*).
- In *yes/no* question forms, *can* changes place with the subject while the main verb doesn't move. *Wh-* question words are placed at the beginning of the question forms.
- The contraction *can't* is usually used in spoken English and increasingly in the written form, except in formal contexts or for emphasis. (The long form negative is one word – *cannot*.)

Pronunciation
Can is usually pronounced /kən/ except when stressed for emphasis when it is pronounced /kæn/. *Can't* is usually pronounced /kɑːnt/.

Vocabulary
Nouns: *back, Chinese, gorilla, month, picture, tennis, tree, week, word, year*
Verbs: *can, climb, crawl, dance, focus, read, ride, say, see, sing, smell, speak, swim, taste, understand, write*
Adjectives: *newborn, one*
Adverb: *clearly*

▶ **Worksheet A**

Student's Book answers
1b 1 ✓ 2 ✗ 3 ✓
  c Yes, they can.
  2 **What can** they do?
    They **can** crawl. They **can't** walk.
    Can they run?
    No, they **can't**.
  3 1 Children can read. Gorillas can't read.
    2 Children can write. Gorillas can't write.
    3 Children can climb trees. Gorillas can climb trees.
    4 Children can run. Gorillas can run.
    5 Children can use a telephone. Gorillas can't use a telephone.

Groupwork suggestion
Write a list of verbs on the board (*run, swim, climb trees*, etc.) and another list of different animals (*elephant, fox, fish, gorilla*, etc.). In groups, students have to use the words on the board to make as many true affirmative and negative statements as they can within a given time.

Student's Book answers
  4 1 Can he speak Chinese?
    2 Can he swim?
    3 Can they play tennis?
    4 Can she sing?
    5 Can she ride a bike?
    6 Can they dance?
  5 1 No, he can't.
    2 No, he can't.
    3 Yes, they can.
    4 Yes, she can.
    5 No, she can't.
    6 Yes, they can.

Pairwork suggestion
Students practise asking each other the questions in exercise 4 and giving short answers. After the practice, check with open pairs or question and answer chain round the class.

Student's Book answers
  6 **What can** you **see**? **Can** you **see** Saturn?
    No, I **can't**. I **can't see** Saturn. I **can see** the back of your head!

▶ **Worksheet B**

Student's Book answers
  7 Answers will vary.

Pairwork suggestion
Students ask each other questions using the verbs in exercise 7 and give short answers. They can then report back to the class on what their partner can and can't do.

Student's Book answers
Puzzle
an old woman and a young woman; a rabbit and a bird

Worksheet

Extra vocabulary: *hear*

A Preteach the verbs as a preview to the unit; mime is a good idea. Students do activity A for consolidation and written record.
  Answers 1 hear 2 smell 3 see 4 taste 5 crawl 6 walk
    7 run 8 climb 9 write 10 understand 11 read
    12 speak

B Students do this activity before activity 7.
  Answers dance – 6, 11 play –2, 7, 9 ride – 1, 8, 10
    sing – 4, 12 swim – 3, 5,

What can you do?

A Match the words with the pictures.

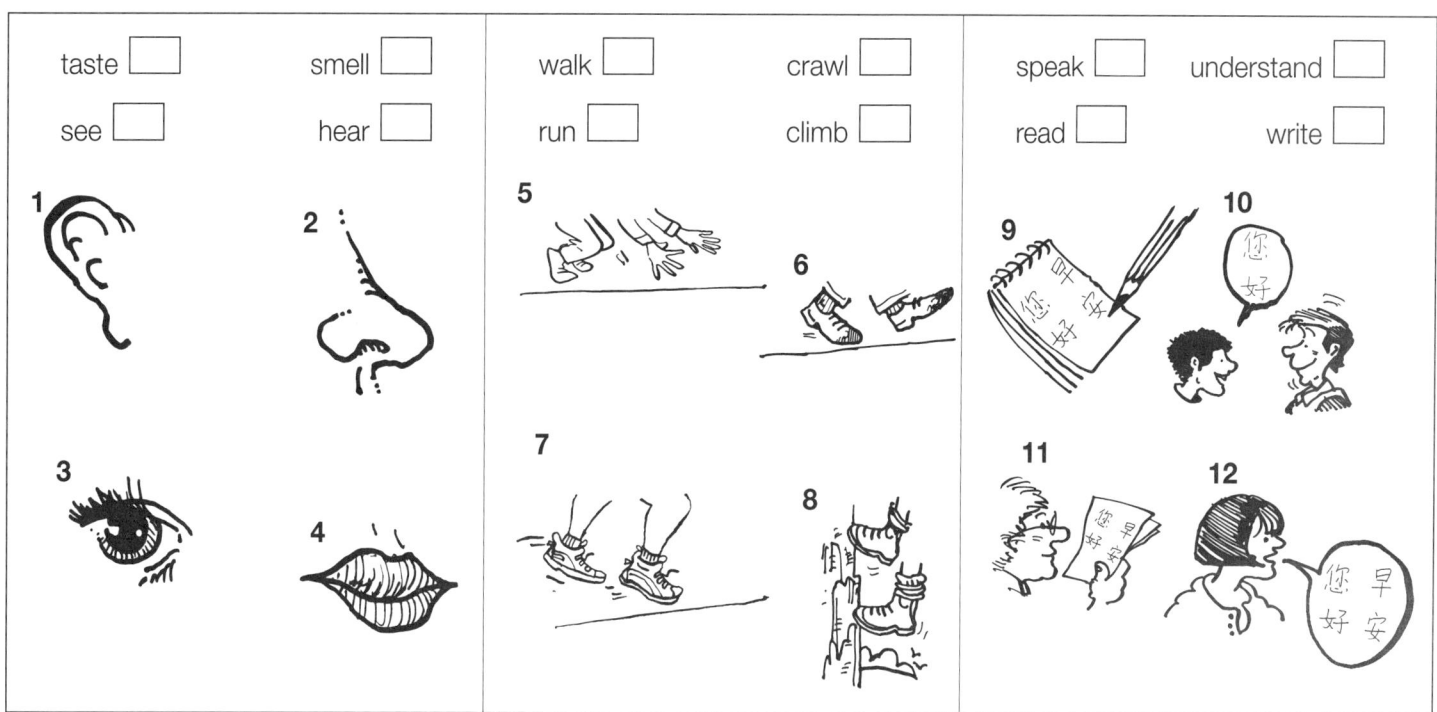

taste ☐ smell ☐

see ☐ hear ☐

walk ☐ crawl ☐

run ☐ climb ☐

speak ☐ understand ☐

read ☐ write ☐

B Choose pictures for each word.

dance ☐ ☐

play ☐ ☐ ☐

ride ☐ ☐ ☐

sing ☐ ☐

swim ☐ ☐

1a 1 Have you got any books in your bag?
2 Have you got an apple (in your bag)?
3 Have you got a dictionary (in your bag)?
4 Have you got any sandwiches (in your bag)?

b 1–4 Yes, I have. / No, I haven't. Answers will vary.

2a 1 Are there any parks?
2 Is there a post office?
3 Are there any shops?
4 Is there a swimming pool?
5 Is there a bank?
6 Are there any restaurants?

b 1 Yes, there are.   2 No, there isn't.   3 Yes, there are.
4 Yes, there is.   5 No, there isn't.   6 No, there aren't.

3 1 How much lemonade is there?
2 How much ice cream is there?
3 How much chicken is there?
4 How many glasses are there?
5 How many sausages are there?
6 How many cakes are there?
7 How much orange juice is there?

4 1 Where's the orange juice?
It's in front of the lemonade.
2 Where are the glasses?
They're next to the chicken.
3 Where's the chicken?
It's between the glasses and the cakes.
4 Where are the sandwiches?
They're on the small table.
5 Where are the sausages?
They're in front of the ice cream.
6 Where's the lemonade?
It's behind the orange juice.

5 1 Don't climb the tree.
2 Don't eat it!
3 Wash your hands.
4 Read your book.
5 Don't sit on the cat!

6 1 Can she swim?   Yes, she can.
2 Can they climb trees?   Yes, they can.
3 Can he read?   No, he can't.
4 Can she draw/write?   No, she can't.
5 Can they sing?   Yes, they can.
6 Can they play computer games?   Yes, they can.

Double check! 7–12

1 1 It hasn't got any hair.
2 It's got two heads.
3 It hasn't got any ears.
4 It's got six eyes.
5 It hasn't got a nose.
6 It's got three arms.
7 It hasn't got any fingers.
8 It's got five legs.
9 It's got five feet.

2 1 It's behind the cup.
2 It's on the cup.
3 It's by/beside/next to the cup.
4 It's between the cups.
5 It's under the cup.

3 1 Eat a sandwich.
2 Go to bed.
3 Drink some water.
4 Run!
5 Wash your face.

4 1 They're in the tree.
2 I can see twenty-one eggs.
3 It's behind a tree.
4 No, they can't.
5 It's under the elephant.
6 There are twelve ducks.

1 Look at the cartoon of the alien from Saturn. Write sentences. Use *have got* and the words below.

1 hair   2 head   3 ears
4 eyes   5 nose
6 arms   7 fingers
8 legs   9 feet

1 *It hasn't got any hair.*

2 _____

3 _____

4 _____

5 _____

6 _____

7 _____

8 _____

9 _____

2 Where's the ball? Write a sentence for each picture.

1 *It's* _____

2 _____

3 _____

4 _____

5 _____

3 Match the sentences on the left with the advice on the right.

1 I'm hungry. •   • Wash your face.

2 I'm tired. •   • Run!

3 I'm hot. •   • Go to bed.

4 I'm late. •   • Eat a sandwich.

5 I'm dirty. •   • Drink some water.

4 Look at the picture of the jungle. Answer the questions. Write sentences.

1 Where are the gorillas?

_____

2 How many eggs can you see?

_____

3 Where's the leopard?

_____

4 Can elephants climb trees?

_____

5 Where's the mouse?

_____

6 How many ducks are there?

13 Papuans live in the Pacific

Present simple *I, you, we, they* affirmative and negative forms

Meaning
Present simple here refers to general time, rather than the specific present moment, and represents ongoing states or repeated actions.

Form
- The auxiliary verb *do*, usually used only in negatives, may cause problems for students. They may either include it in the affirmative (which is only used for strong emphasis/contradiction) or omit it in the negative: * *I do live*, * *I no live*, * *I not live*.
- The negative is almost always contracted in both spoken and written English except for emphasis or in very formal situations.

Vocabulary
Nouns: *baseball, blood, bus, camel, cereal, coconut, cowboy, desert, football, forest, guitar, language, model, mosquito, motorbike, mountain, musical instrument, necklace, Pacific, parents, pizza, road, sea, stamp, stone, tent, vegetable, village*
Verbs: *collect, drive, fish, fly, go, grow, hunt, keep, learn, like, live, make, paint, watch*
Adjectives: *big, special*
Countries, nationalities and people: *America – American(s), Australia – Australian(s), Brazil – Brazilian(s), Britain – British, Canada – Canadian(s), Italy – Italian(s), Mongolia – Mongolian(s)/Mongol(s), Papua (New Guinea) – Papuan(s)*

Preview activity
Students look at the illustrations with the presentation text. Ask them *Where is it?* and to name any things in the picture that they know in English (*axe, fish, people, bananas* etc.).

Student's Book answers
1b 1 C ✗ 2 A ✓ 3 B ✗
2a + They **live** in villages.
  – They **don't live** in cities.
  b + They **wear** necklaces.
  – They **don't wear** school uniforms.

Pairwork suggestion
Working from the text, pairs of students find three more present simple sentences and copy these out removing the verb. Each pair exchanges sentences with another pair. Pairs try to replace the missing verbs *without* looking at the text.

Student's Book answers
3 1 Papuans don't eat hamburgers.
 2 Americans like baseball.
 3 Canadians don't grow bananas.
 4 Italians eat pizzas.
 5 Brazilians grow coffee.
 6 Papuans don't speak Italian.

Worksheet **A** and **B**

Pair/Groupwork suggestion
In pairs/groups, students write their own sentences on a 'round the world' theme. They jumble their sentences and exchange them with other pairs/groups to solve. If this is the first time the students have met the material, rather than this being a feedback for the whole unit, they may need more help with their sentences.

Student's Book answers
4 1 eat, drink 2 don't go, listen 3 don't live, live 4 live, don't drive, ride

Pairwork suggestion
In pairs, students secretly choose one or more nationalities and write sentences. They use the verbs from the box, their own nouns and *they*. Pairs read out their sentences to the class until the identity of the nationality is guessed or the answer must be given.

Student's Book answers
5 1 Mosquitoes don't eat chips. They drink blood.
 2 Cowboys don't drive buses. They ride horses.
 3 Fish don't fly in the sky. They swim in the sea.
 4 I don't speak a Papuan language. I speak …

Pairwork suggestion
In pairs, students write three sets of sentences of their own, similar in structure to *Mosquitoes don't eat chips. They drink blood.* (Encourage amusing content.) Each half set (e.g. *Mosquitoes don't eat chips.*) is written on a separate piece of paper. Collect all the pieces of paper and redistribute them. Students read their half sets to each other and match up the sets.

Student's Book answers
6 1 collect stamps 2 make models 3 play football
 4 read comics 5 ride a motorbike 6 watch TV
7 Answers will vary.

Classwork suggestion
Write three verbs on the board, e.g. *play, ride, drive*. Students then add as many appropriate nouns as they can around the verbs. These can then be expanded orally in sentences. You can focus attention on verb sets which cause problems, e.g. *clean/wash; wear/carry; watch/see/look at; say/tell/speak*, etc.

Student's Book answers
Puzzle
'Babs and I don't play a musical instrument' is the key information and where to start. The rest is elimination.

Al – drums; Clare – guitar; Dave – stamps; Babs – models

Poster project suggestion
In groups, students choose a country that interests them. They draw a map of the country, including labelled geographical features (*mountains, rivers*, etc.). They illustrate the map with either drawings or pictures from magazines of aspects of life there and write captions in English.

Worksheet

Extra vocabulary: *Argentina, Chile, China, Greece, India, Japan, Mexico, New Zealand, Portugal, Spain, Thailand, Turkey, United States of America*

A and B Use these activities after exercise 3. You can use the map to teach the countries listed. Then ask students to complete the list for written record.

Vocabulary extension activity You can use the map to teach further countries, adjectives and languages that you think are most appropriate for your students at this stage. Example: *Britain, British, English; Brazil, Brazilian, Portuguese.*

A Look at the map and write the names of the countries in your language.

Japan

Papua New Guinea

Australia

New Zealand

Mongolia

China

Thailand

India

Italy

Britain

Spain

Portugal

Greece

Turkey

Argentina

Brazil

Chile

Canada

Mexico

United States of America

Argentina _____

Australia _____

Brazil _____

Britain _____

Canada _____

Chile _____

China _____

Greece _____

India _____

Italy _____

Japan _____

Mexico _____

Mongolia _____

New Zealand _____

Papua New Guinea _____

Portugal _____

Spain _____

Thailand _____

Turkey _____

United States of America _____

B Add four countries to the list. Use a dictionary and write the names of the countries in English.

_____

_____

_____

_____

From **GRAMMAR WORKS 1** by Mick Gammidge
© Cambridge University Press 1998

PHOTOCOPIABLE

33

14 Do you play the drums?

Present simple *I, you, we, they* question forms
Where, when, what, how
Prepositions of time *at, in, on*

Present simple: Meaning
- Present simple in this unit is used with the same reference as in Unit 13, for general time.

Form
- The question words are placed at the beginning of questions before the auxiliary verb, which is *do* unless the verb is *be*.
- Because students have already been introduced to *have got*, they may put *have* as an auxiliary in the present simple but *have* is usually used as a main verb with *do* in the present simple, e.g. *Do you have a pen*? rather than *Have you a pen*?
- In short answers, *do/don't* must be the last word of the reply, without the main verb, e.g. *Yes, I do*. not **Yes, I do speak*.

Pronunciation
The pronunciation of the auxiliary *do* in question forms is /də/. In spoken English, *do you* is often pronounced /djuː/. In short answers, *do* as the final word is pronounced fully: /duː/ and is stressed.

Prepositions
Prepositions of time do not show the same clear meanings as prepositions of place, but they are regular in that they collocate with the time nouns used:
- **in** seasons: spring, summer, autumn, winter
  periods of day: morning, afternoon, evening (but, **at** night)
- **on** days: Monday, New Year's Day, my birthday
- **at** hour of day: 9.30, ten o'clock
  weekends
  general periods of festivals: New Year

Vocabulary
Nouns: *aeroplane, basketball, class, country, drum kit, drums, English, evening, food, French, history, lunch, maths, morning, neighbour, piano, science, uncle, walk, wall*
Verbs: *come, get up, know, practise, start, study, think, tidy*
Adjectives: *cold, terrible*
Prepositions of time: *at, in, on*
Days of the week: *Monday, Tuesday, Wednesday, Thursday, Friday, Saturday, Sunday*
Seasons: *spring, summer, autumn, winter*
Months: *July, August*
Wh- question words: *how, when*

Student's Book answers
1b 3 1 2

Comprehension check suggestion
Ask students *Do Kim's neighbours like the drums?*

Student's Book answers
2a 1 Yes, I do.
   2 I go to school in London.
   3 I go to school in the morning.
   4 I walk to school.
   5 I study science.
 b 1 **Do** you get up at 7.00? No, I **don't**.
   2 **When do** you get up? I **get up** at 6.00.

3 1 Do you drive a car?
   2 Do you listen to the radio?
   3 Do you study English?
   4 Do you do (your) homework?
   5 Do you sing songs?
   6 Do you play the piano?
4 Yes, I do. / No, I don't. Answers will vary.

▶ *Worksheet* **A** and **B**

Classwork suggestion
Exercise 3 can be expanded into a class questionnaire. Pairs/groups ask the questions in exercise 3, or different questions made from the words in Worksheet activity A, to everyone in the class and collect the answers. The answers can be used to recycle *How many … ? (How many people play the piano? Five people in the class play the piano.)* Results can be collated and displayed in a bar chart.

Student's Book answers
5a in – the morning   on – Monday   at – 1.00/2.00
 b 1 at 2 at 3 at 4 in 5 in 6 At 7 On 8 in 9 in
6 1 Where do you go to school?
   2 When do you start class?
   3 How do you go to school?
   4 What do you study?
   5 Do you have tests?
   6 When do you do your homework?
   7 Do you like homework?
7 Answers will vary.

Pairwork suggestion
In pairs, students ask each other questions from the present simple charts in the **Grammar reference**, page 68 and give true answers, e.g. A: *Do you study English?* B: *Yes, I do.* A: *When do you study English?* B: *I study English … .*

Pairwork suggestion
Students practise asking and answering the questions in exercise 6.

Student's Book answers
Puzzle
They sing songs.
The first letter of the verb is the same as the first letter of the day!

Worksheet

Extra vocabulary: *donkey, geography*

A and B You can use the pictures in activity A to revise/preteach the nouns for the numbered illustrations after exercise 4. Students then complete the labels for written record.

Answers 1 baseball 2 basketball 3 bike 4 camel 5 camera
      6 computer 7 computer games 8 donkey 9 drums
      10 English 11 football 12 geography 13 guitar
      14 history 15 horse 16 knife and fork 17 maths
      18 motorbike 19 piano 20 science 21 telephone

Students then do activity B. They write the nouns in activity A with the appropriate verbs in the diagrams.

Answers play baseball, basketball, computer games, drums, football, guitar, piano
      ride bike, camel, donkey, horse, motorbike
      study English, geography, history, maths, science
      use camera, computer, knife and fork, telephone

Do you play the drums?

A What are these things? Write words for the pictures.

1 _____

2 _____

3 _____

4 _____

5 _____

6 _____

7 _____

8 _donkey_____

9 _____

10 _____

11 _____

12 _geography__

13 _____

14 _history____

15 _____

16 ___ and ____

17 _maths_____

18 _____

19 _____

20 _____

21 _____

B Write the nouns from activity A with the correct verbs.

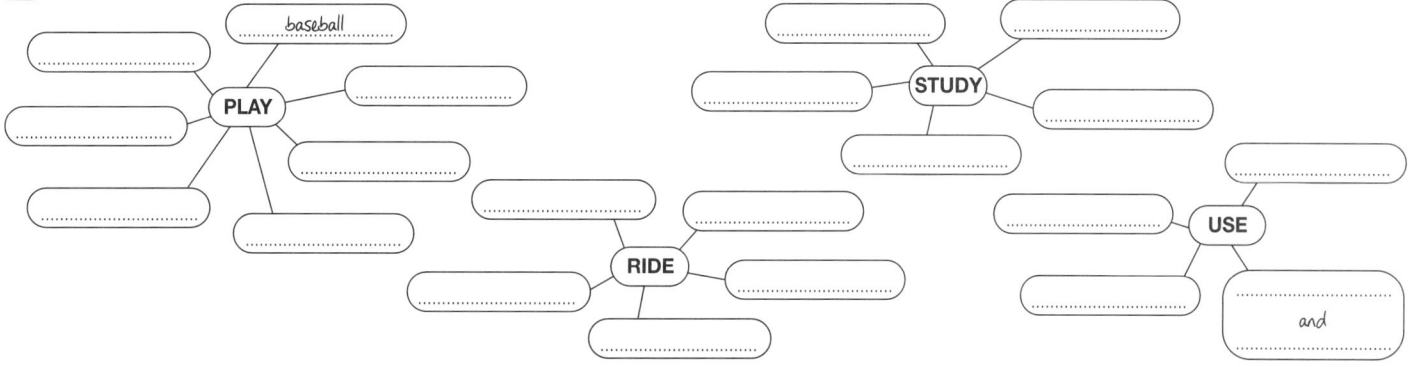

PLAY — baseball

STUDY

RIDE

USE — and

15 *Sometimes he doesn't wake up for school*

Present simple third person
Adverbs of frequency

Present simple
Present simple third person -*s* is introduced here. The spelling and pronunciation rules are the same as for plural endings of nouns (see Unit 3). In negative and question forms, the third person ending attaches to *do* (*does*) and the main verb stays in the infinitive form.

Adverbs
Adverbs of frequency come before the main verb (except with *be* where they come after). *Usually* and *sometimes* can also be placed before the subject. (Some of these adverbs can also occur at the ends of sentences but this can be avoided at this level.)

Vocabulary
Verbs: *brush, carry, cook, help, meet, take care of, wake up*
Nouns: *cinema, housework, husband, jogging, journey, shopping*
Adverbs: *always, never, often, rarely, sometimes, usually*
Adjective: *hard*

▶ *Worksheet* **A and B**
Student's Book answers
1c 1 takes   2 doesn't
2b watches   tidies   reads   does
3 1 She doesn't eat vegetables. She eats burgers.
  2 She doesn't read newspapers. She reads comics.
  3 She studies English. She doesn't study Chinese.
  4 She doesn't watch football on TV. She watches music.
4 1 Does she eat burgers?   Yes, she does.
  2 Does she read comics?   Yes, she does.
  3 Does she study Chinese?   No, she doesn't.
  4 Does she watch football?   No, she doesn't.
5 100% always   sometimes   0% never
6 1 She sometimes goes to the cinema.
  2 She often meets her friends.
  3 She never goes jogging.
  4 She rarely tidies her bedroom.
  5 She usually listens to the radio.
  6 She always brushes her teeth.

Classwork suggestion
Play 'Find someone who ...'. Each student thinks of three unusual things they do at weekends, e.g. write letters. They write questions about these three activities which they then ask the other students, e.g. *Do you write letters at weekends?* Students reply using adverbs of frequency, e.g. *I never write letters at weekends*. When students find someone who does the activity (however infrequently), they record that student's name and answer. When all students have found someone for all their questions, they report back to the class, e.g. *Peter sometimes writes letters at weekends*.

Student's Book answers
7 Answers will vary.

Classwork suggestion
Place two chairs in the middle of the room. One student sits on each chair. The class asks one student questions but she/he must remain silent while the second student answers for her/him. The first student then says if the answers are correct or not. (Q1: *Do you play football?* S2: *No, she doesn't.* S1: *Wrong. Yes, I do.*) Alternatively, or as an extension, one chair can be out in the middle and left empty. The class chooses a famous person and puts questions to the empty chair. The class provides likely answers.

Classwork suggestion
Play 'Twenty Questions'. To make the game easier, first of all choose a category such as animals or famous people. One student thinks of something/someone from the category without saying what/who it is. The other students have to ask *yes/no* questions to find out what/who it is, and they must guess the answer within twenty questions. (This is a good opportunity to practise other language like *can, have got, be*, etc. as well as the present simple.)

Student's Book answers
Puzzle
80 minutes = 1 hour and 20 minutes; so the journey takes the same time in both cars!

Worksheet

Extra vocabulary: *clothes, put on*

A and B   Preteach the items as a preview to the unit; mime is a good idea. Students then do the activity for written record.
Answers   1 n   2 c   3 l   4 i   5 h   6 m   7 k   8 e   9 j
           10 f   11 d   12 o   13 g   14 b   15 a

Students then do activity B. Ask questions that are relevant to the text about Chris Herbert, e.g. *Do you help your parents? Do you go to the shops? Do you cook? Do you wash the dishes? Do you take care of your brothers and sisters?*

A Match the phrases with the pictures.

a ☐ b ☐ c ☐ d ☐ e ☐ f ☐ g ☐ h ☐ i ☐ j ☐ k ☐ l ☐ m ☐ n [1] o ☐

1 brush your hair ☐	**6** get up ☐	**11** put on your clothes ☐
2 brush your teeth ☐	**7** go jogging ☐	**12** take care of a pet ☐
3 carry the shopping ☐	**8** go to the cinema ☐	**13** tidy your bedroom ☐
4 cook food ☐	**9** help your brothers or sisters with their homework ☐	**14** wake up ☐
5 eat breakfast ☐	**10** meet friends ☐	**15** wash ☐

B What do you do every day? Tick (✓) or cross (✗) the phrases in activity A.

She hates speaking English

Object pronouns
Like, love, enjoy, hate + -ing form

Pronoun
Object pronouns may cause some confusion in that some are the same in form as subject pronouns, while some are different.

-ing form
The *-ing* form introduced here is the gerund which acts as a noun. The gerund can act as either subject or object, though here it is only introduced in object position. (The *-ing* form as present participle appears in the next unit, Unit 17, in the present continuous.)

Spelling
- For verbs ending in more than one consonant or ending in more than one vowel and then one consonant, add *-ing*, e.g. *watching, cooking*.
- For verbs ending in one vowel and one consonant, double the consonant and add *-ing*, e.g. *swimming*. Note that verbs ending in the consonants *-w, -y* or *-x* do not follow this rule and these consonants do not double. With verbs of more than one syllable this rule becomes more complex. When the stress is on the last syllable the final consonant doubles, e.g. *beginning*. Where the stress is not on the final syllable, then the final consonant is not doubled, e.g. *listening*. However, there are some irregular verbs that do not follow these rules, e.g. *travelling*.
- For verbs ending in *-e* drop the *-e* and add *-ing*, e.g. *making*.
- For verbs ending in *-ie*, change *-ie* to *-y* and add *-ing*.

Vocabulary
Verbs: *answer, ask, clean, die, enjoy, give, hate, lie, love, telephone, tie, visit, want*
Adjective: *mad,*
Nouns: *beach, carnival, grandma, grandmother, information, letter, professor, project, South America*
Object pronouns: *her, him, it, me, them, us, you*
Determiner: *every*

Student's Book answers
1b 1 ✗   2 ✓   3 ✗   4 ✓   5 ✗
2b she – her   he – him   it – it   they – them
3 1 them   2 us   3 you   4 her   5 them   6 it, me

Groupwork suggestion
In groups of about six, students play a knockout game in a circle. The first student says a subject pronoun (*he, she, it,* etc.) and the second student gives the corresponding object pronoun and then another subject pronoun, and so on round the circle. If a student gives the wrong answer or hesitates, they are out of the circle. The game continues until only one student is left. (You may wish to set a time limit for this.)

Student's Book answers
4a dancing – dance   lying – lie   swimming – swim   singing – sing
b Words ending in:
  • *-e*: -̶e̶ + *-ing*
  • *-ie*: -̶i̶e̶ + *-y* + *-ing*
  • a vowel and then a consonant, (e.g. *-ut, -un, -it*), double – × 2 – the consonant + *-ing*
  • Other words: + *-ing*
c speak – speaking   take – taking   die – dying   run – running
  wash – washing   make – making   tie – tying   put – putting

5 1 He hates getting up.
2 She hates using the computer.
3 They enjoy/like/love walking.
4 She enjoys/likes/loves shopping.
5 They enjoy/like/love eating.
6 He enjoys/likes/loves lying in bed.

Further practice suggestion
Refer students to the verb/noun sets in Unit 13, exercise 6 and Unit 14, exercise 3 and ask them to write sentences about themselves using *like, love, enjoy, don't like, hate,* e.g. *I enjoy watching TV.*

Classwork suggestion
Play 'Find someone who …'. Tell students to write down an interesting *like/love/hate/enjoy* + verb combination, e.g. *like getting up early / hate singing,* on a piece of paper. Encourage students to be creative. Collect the papers and redistribute them. Tell students they are to stand up, move round and find someone who answers *yes* to the question they make from the words on the paper, e.g. *Do you like getting up early?* When everyone has a name of someone who has answered *yes,* students tell the class, using the third person, e.g. *Elena likes getting up early.*

Student's Book answers
6 1 them   2 her   3 studying   4 writing   5 me   6 reading
  7 us   8 you
7 Answers will vary.
Puzzle
The professor loves verbs with **an** in them!

▶ *Worksheet*

Worksheet
Use this activity at the end of the unit for revision of verbs + *-ing* form. Students complete the worksheet for consolidation and written record.
Answers   1 singing   2 dancing   3 lying   4 eating   5 walking
  6 taking   7 making   8 painting   9 getting up
  10 running   11 cleaning   12 shopping   13 swimming
  14 washing   15 tidying   16 wearing

She hates speaking English

Write the *-ing* form of the verbs.

She loves ...

She hates ...

1 _____ singing _____

9 _____

2 _____

10 _____

3 _____ in bed

11 _____

4 _____

12 _____

5 _____

13 _____

6 _____ the dog for a walk

14 _____ the dishes

7 _____ models

15 _____ her bedroom

8 _____

16 _____ a hat

From **Grammar Works 1** by Mick Gammidge
© Cambridge University Press 1998

17 They're standing up and shouting

Present continuous

Meaning

The present continuous has many uses, but here it is used for actions in progress now and around now. It is not usually used for stative verbs (e.g. *be, love, like, know*) which talk about a state/condition rather than an action. Stative verbs generally take a simple tense. Similarly, verbs of sense (e.g. *smell, see, taste, hear*) also generally use *can* rather than the continuous form, except when we are talking about deliberate actions.

Form

- The present continuous is formed using the auxiliary verb *be* and the present participle of the verb (an *-ing* form with the same spelling rules as the gerund: see Unit 16). Questions are made by inverting the subject and auxiliary while the main verb doesn't move.
- Short answers don't use the main verb, and end with the auxiliary.
- In the affirmative and negative, the auxiliary verb *be* is generally contracted in spoken English except for emphasis or in formal contexts. In written English, the full form is used except in informal contexts, such as letters to friends.

Vocabulary

Verbs: *draw, feel, look, shout, stand up*
Nouns: *board, clothes, coat, dinner, game, goal, officer, police, stadium*
Adjective: *long*
Other words: *goodbye, past*

▶ **Worksheet**

Student's Book answers

1b 1 B   2 D   3 A   4 C
2 1 Are, playing   2 Is, isn't, She's listening   3 Are, are
3 1 I'm painting a picture.
   2 You're sitting on my coat.
   3 You aren't wearing your school uniform.
   4 Look! He's walking.
   5 You aren't doing your homework.
   6 They aren't eating their dinner.

Groupwork suggestion

In groups of at least three, S1 gives an instruction to S2, e.g. *Please play the piano*. S3 comments: *She/He's playing the piano*. S2 then gives an instruction to S3: *Please brush your teeth*. S3 mimes brushing her/his teeth and S4 says *She/He's brushing her/his teeth*, and so on round the group.

Student's Book answers

4 1 She's dancing.
   2 She's writing on the board.
   3 They're drawing.
   4 He's playing a computer game.
   5 They're reading a comic.
5 1 Are you dancing?
      No, I'm not. I'm tidying the books.
   2 Are you writing on the board?
      No, I'm not. I'm cleaning it.
   3 Are you drawing?
      No, we're not. We're writing.
   4 Are you playing a computer game?
      No, I'm not. I'm using a calculator.
   5 Are you reading a comic?
      No, we're not. We're studying.

Groupwork suggestion

In groups, students take it in turns to mime an action or activity, e.g. swimming, washing their hands. Members of the group ask questions, e.g. *Are you swimming?* and the person miming answers, *No, I'm not. / Yes, I am.* When the mime is guessed, another student mimes their action. After practising, groups can compete against each other, e.g. a member from one group mimes their activity and members of the other groups take it in turns to ask questions. A running score for correct answers can be kept on the board.

Student's Book answers

6 1 'm telephoning   2 's riding   3 's wearing   4 's carrying
   5 's   6 aren't listening
7 Answers will vary.

Pairwork suggestion

Students practise asking and answering the questions in exercise 7 in pairs.

Student's Book answers

Puzzle
670 books – 7% of students have one book, half the remainder have two books and the other half have no books – which equals one book for each student.

Worksheet

Extra vocabulary: *fishing, riding, skating, skiing, table tennis, volleyball*

Use this activity as a preview to the unit. Preteach the new sports: *skiing, volleyball, table tennis*. (Students should be able to work out *fishing, riding* and *skating* from the verb forms.) Students then do the activity for consolidation and written record.

Answers   1 volleyball   2 football   3 tennis   4 basketball
   5 fishing   6 baseball   7 riding   8 swimming
   9 skating   10 skiing   11 table tennis

Write the words with the pictures.

baseball   basketball   fishing   football   riding   skating   skiing   swimming   table tennis   tennis   ~~volleyball~~

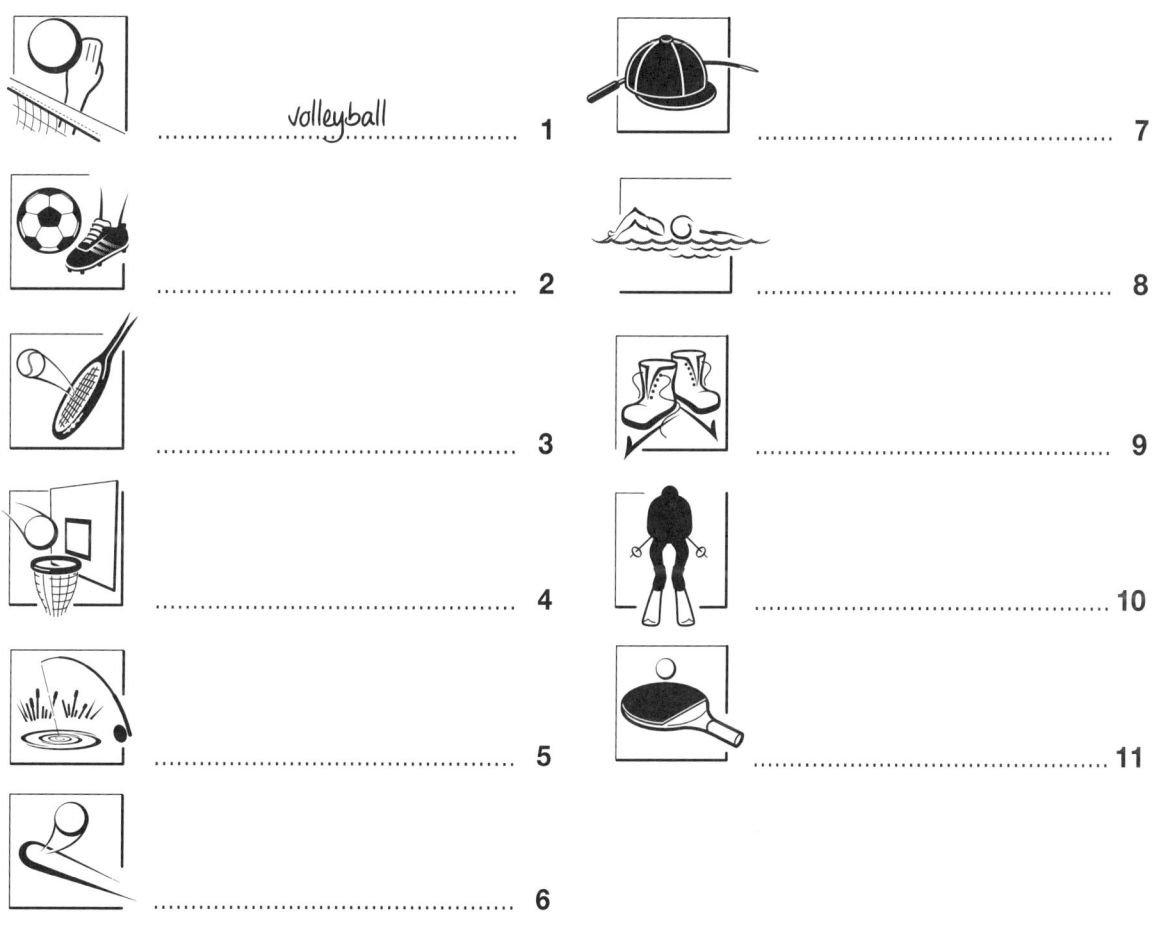

SPORTS WORLD

..........volleyball.......... **1**

.... **2**

.... **3**

.... **4**

.... **5**

.... **6**

.... **7**

.... **8**

.... **9**

.... **10**

.... **11**

From **GRAMMAR WORKS 1** by Mick Gammidge
© Cambridge University Press 1998

PHOTOCOPIABLE

41

18 What is James doing?

Present simple and present continuous contrast
What ... ?

Meaning
- In this unit, the present simple is contrasted with the present continuous. Here, the present continuous refers to actions happening now and the present simple refers to general time. Compare *I eat ice cream* (usually but not at this moment) and *I'm eating ice cream* (now).

Form
- Note that *What do you do?*, practised in exercise 6, usually means *What is your job?*, but this depends on the situation.
- Students need to know that stative verbs (e.g. *know, want, love, like, hate*) which describe states or conditions, rather than actions, do not usually take continuous tenses. For stative verbs, simple tenses are usually used.
- Verbs of sense (e.g. *smell, see, hear, taste*) usually take *can* rather than the present continuous.

Vocabulary
Nouns: *dentist, doctor, eclipse, father, moon, planet, sky, tonight*
Verbs: *check, sleep, stay up, wait*
Adverb: *before*
Adjective: *on fire*

Preview activity
Ask students to look at the picture with the presentation text. Ask *Who is it? (James.) What is he doing? (He's watching the moon.) What is he using? (A telescope.) What's the picture on the poster? (An eclipse.)*

▶ Worksheet A
Student's Book answers
1b 1 looks   2 is looking
 c looks   is looking
2a 1 What is James doing?
 2 Where is James sitting?
 b 1 He's looking at the moon.
 2 He's sitting in his bedroom.

3b | present simple | present continuous |
| --- | --- |
| I study | I'm studying |
| you study | you're studying |
| she studies | she's studying |
| he studies | he's studying |
| it studies | it's studying |
| we study | we're studying |
| they study | they're studying |

4 1 likes   2 isn't listening   3 is thinking   4 knows
 5 watches   6 knows   7 does ... know   8 is sleeping
5 1 What are you doing?
 2 I'm cooking.
 3 What are you cooking?
 4 What do you want?
 5 Where are your cassettes?
 6 Where are you going?
6 1 What are you doing?   I'm looking at his teeth.
  What do you do?   I'm a dentist.
 2 What do you do?   I'm a doctor.
  What are you doing?   I'm looking at your eyes.
 3 What are you doing?   I'm brushing the horse.
  What do you do?   I'm a farmer.

▶ Worksheet B
Groupwork suggestion
Bring to class magazine pictures of people engaged in activities, e.g. street scenes, sports arenas, offices, hospitals. Students write descriptions of the people and the actions. Encourage them to make guesses about the people's occupations.

Student's Book answers
7   Answers will vary.

Pairwork suggestion
Students practise asking and answering the questions in exercise 7 in pairs.

Student's Book answers
Puzzle
His son.

Worksheet

Extra vocabulary: *artist, comet, painter, police officer, space, student*

A   Use this activity as a preview to the unit. Ask students to look at the poster. Ask them to name the items they know (*sun, star*). Then use the poster to elicit or preteach *moon, eclipse, comet, space, planet*. Ask students *Do you watch the stars/planets?* With monolingual groups in their own country you could ask students in their own language if they have ever seen an eclipse. Students then do the activity for written record.
 Answers   1 moon   2 stars   3 comet   4 sun   5 planets
       6 space

B   Use this activity to practise vocabulary after exercise 6. Ask students to look at the pictures. Point to a picture and ask *What does she/he do? (She/He's an artist.)* Students can practise asking and answering questions about all the pictures in pairs. They then complete the word square and write the words with the pictures.
 Answers   1 artist   2 painter   3 doctor   4 teacher   5 farmer
       6 singer   7 police officer   8 dentist   9 actor
       10 student

M	R	J	D	S	P	A	I	N	T	E	R	T	A
P	N	U	E	X	K	D	O	F	R	X	T	I	C
T	O	L	N	F	P	L	N	A	R	T	I	S	T
Q	D	A	T	P	S	T	U	D	E	N	T	Z	O
P	O	L	I	C	E	■	O	F	F	I	C	E	R
L	C	P	S	U	J	L	S	A	N	T	S	V	L
S	T	K	T	C	E	I	A	R	Q	S	I	P	T
F	O	J	O	M	P	F	N	M	W	T	J	S	M
E	R	W	R	G	I	K	T	E	A	C	H	E	R
V	Z	Q	S	I	N	G	E	R	F	G	A	W	N

What is James doing?

Worksheet 18

A *Write the words on the poster.*

comet moon planet space star sun

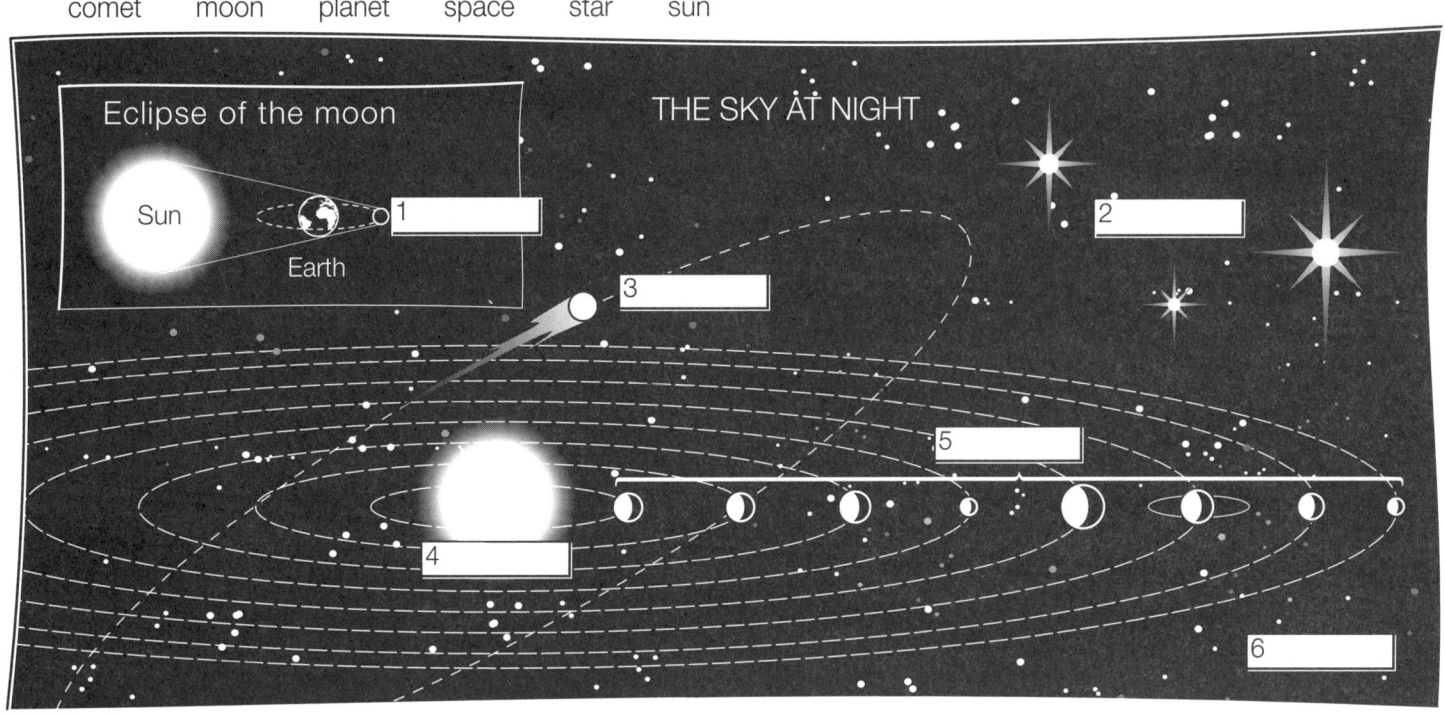

B *Find ten jobs in the word square. Then write the words with the pictures.*

M	R	J	D	S	P	A	I	N	T	E	R	T	A
P	N	U	E	X	K	D	O	F	R	X	T	I	C
T	O	L	N	F	P	L	N	A	R	T	I	S	T
Q	D	A	T	P	S	T	U	D	E	N	T	Z	O
P	O	L	I	C	E	■	O	F	F	I	C	E	R
L	C	P	S	U	J	L	S	A	N	T	S	V	L
S	T	K	T	C	E	I	A	R	Q	S	I	P	T
F	O	J	O	M	P	F	N	M	W	T	J	S	M
E	R	W	R	G	I	K	T	E	A	C	H	E	R
V	Z	Q	S	I	N	G	E	R	F	G	A	W	N

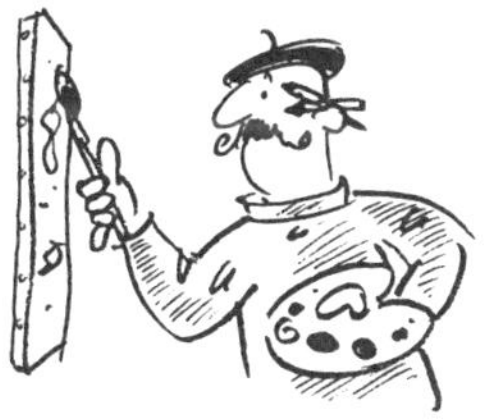

1 artist

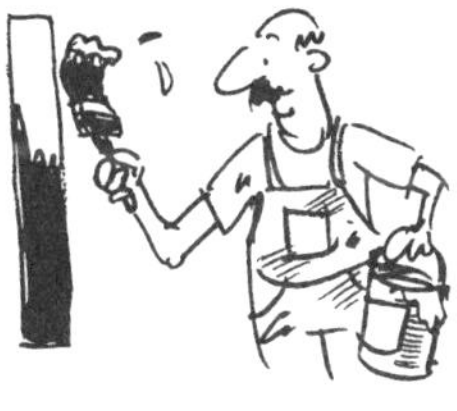

2 ______________

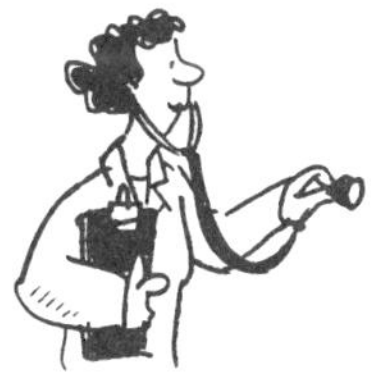

3 ______________

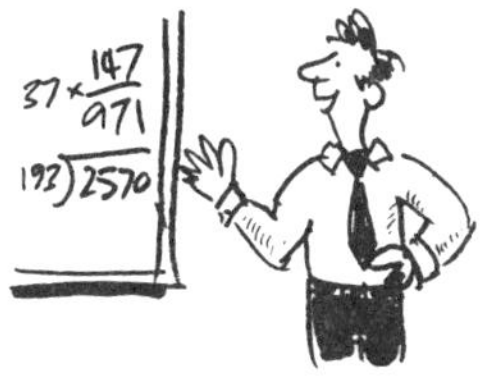

4 ______________

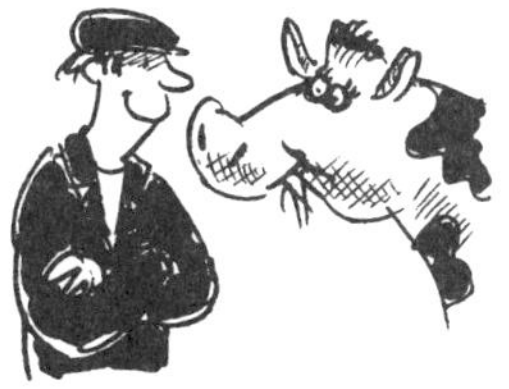

5 ______________

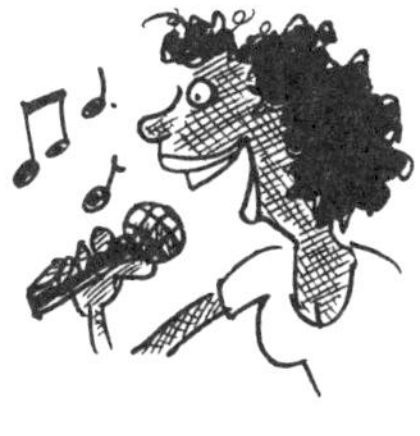

6 ______________

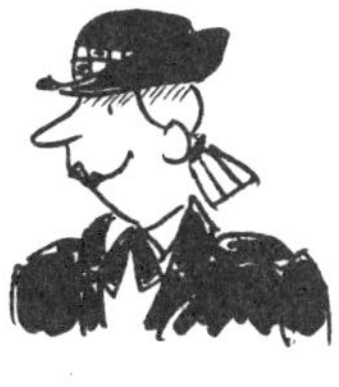

7 ______________

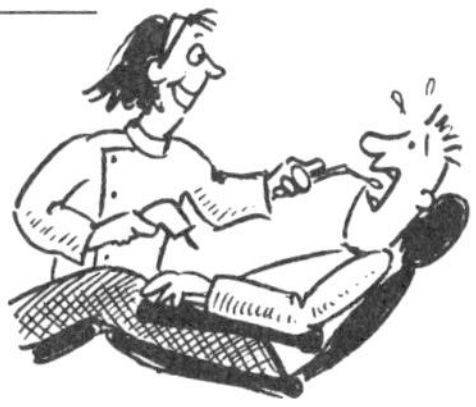

8 ______________

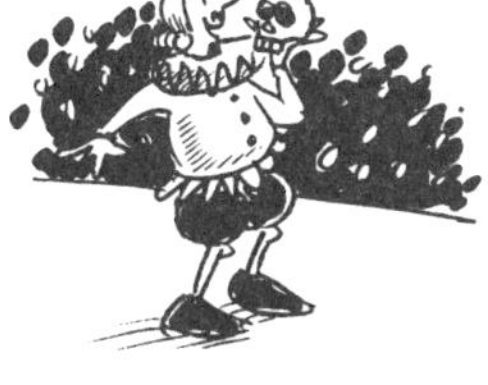

9 ______________

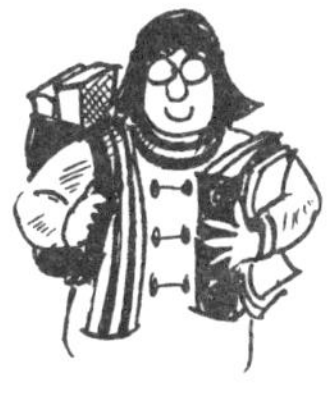

10 ______________

1 1 studies … on
    2 eats … in
    3 studies … on … at
    4 plays … on … in
    5 studies … at … on

2 1 always wins 2 rarely win 3 often wins 4 usually win
    5 sometimes wins 6 never wins

3 1 **When do** we **sleep**? At night.
    2 **Where do** we **buy** magazines? At a newsagent.
    3 **What do** English people **eat** for breakfast? Bacon and eggs, toast or cereal.
    4 **How do** we **learn** new words? We use a dictionary.
    5 **Where do** gorillas **live**? In Africa.
    6 **When do** we **get up**? In the morning.

4

I	my	mine	me
you	your	yours	you
she	her	hers	her
he	his	his	him
it	its	~~its~~	it
Kim	Kim's	Kim's	Kim
the cat	the cat's	the cat's	the cat
we	our	ours	us
they	their	theirs	them
the cats	the cats'	the cats'	the cats

5 Answers will vary.
    1 I like, hate, etc. … / don't like playing football.
    2 I _____ eating sweets.
    3 My friend _____s / doesn't like studying maths.
    4 My mother _____s / doesn't like washing the dishes.
    5 I _____ / don't like tidying my bedroom.
    6 My teacher _____s / doesn't like speaking English.
    7 I _____ / don't like sitting in the sun.
    8 My grandparents _____ / don't like watching TV.
    9 My father _____s / doesn't like going to work.

6 1 What are they doing? They're dancing.
    2 What is it doing? It's sleeping.
    3 What is he doing? He's getting up.
    4 What is she doing? She's reading (a magazine).
    5 What are they doing? They're playing football.
    6 What is she doing? She's eating (an ice cream).
    7 What are they doing? They're listening to the radio.

Double check! 13–18

1 Carlos:
    1 He always does his homework.
    2 He always wears his school uniform.
    3 He always listens to his teacher.
    4 He never plays computer games.
    5 He never eats sweets.
    6 He never runs in the classroom.
    Linda and Mark:
    1 They never do their homework.
    2 They never wear their school uniform.
    3 They never listen to their teacher.
    4 They always play computer games.
    5 They always eat sweets.
    6 They always run in the classroom.

2 a She likes watching TV.
    b She doesn't like reading comics.
    c She hates collecting stamps.
    d She likes taking photos.
    e She likes listening to the radio.
    f She loves going to the cinema.

3 1 goes 2 plays 3 is visiting 4 paints 5 enjoys
    6 is working 7 is helping 8 are painting 9 listens
    10 is using 11 is using 12 isn't enjoying

1 Read the school rules. Then write sentences about the students. Use *always* and *never*.

Carlos is a good student.

1 He always _____

2 _____

3 _____

4 He never _____

5 _____

6 _____

<table>
<tr><td colspan="2"><u>SCHOOL RULES</u></td></tr>
<tr><td>1 Do your homework.</td><td>4 Don't play computer games.</td></tr>
<tr><td>2 Wear your school uniform.</td><td>5 Don't eat sweets.</td></tr>
<tr><td>3 Listen to your teacher.</td><td>6 Don't run in the classroom.</td></tr>
</table>

Linda and Mark are bad students.

1 _____

2 _____

3 _____

4 _____

5 _____

6 _____

2 Look at Sue's answers to the questions. Write sentences about her.

WHAT DO YOU LIKE DOING?

1 = hate   2 = don't like   3 = like   4 = love

		1	2	3	4	
a	TV	1	2	(3)	4	a She likes watching TV.
b	comics	1	(2)	3	4	b _____
c	stamps	(1)	2	3	4	c _____
d	photos	1	2	(3)	4	d _____
e	radio	1	2	(3)	4	e _____
f	cinema	1	2	3	(4)	f _____

3 Complete the text. Use the present simple or the present continuous.

On Saturday afternoons, Carlos usually _____ (1 go) to the park. He _____ (2 play) football with his friends.

But today, he _____ (3 visit) his uncle Jim. Jim is a painter. He _____ (4 paint) houses and he

_____ (5 enjoy) painting. He _____ (6 work) today and Paulo _____ (7 help) him. They

_____ (8 paint) a kitchen. But Carlos never _____ (9 listen) to his uncle. Jim _____ (10 use)

green paint. Carlos _____ (11 use) red paint! Jim _____ (12 not enjoy) painting today.

19 You're going to be busy!

Be + going to + verb affirmative and negative forms

Meaning

Going to is a common future form in English, and has many uses. This unit looks at three uses:

– saying that something is about to happen, either intentionally or accidentally, based on present evidence. Often we can see the action actually starting.
– talking about intentions.
– making general predictions.

Form

- The construction uses the auxiliary verb *be* plus *going to* plus the infinitive without *to*.
- The auxiliary *be* is generally contracted in spoken English except for emphasis or in formal contexts. In written English, the full form is generally used except in informal situations.

Pronunciation

To in *going to* is generally pronounced /tə/.

Vocabulary

Nouns: *colour, free time, life, phone, weekend, window*
Verbs: *break, catch, fall, go out, jump, kick, open, throw*
Adjectives: *green, interesting, lucky, shy*

Preview suggestion

Bring in a horoscope page from a magazine or draw some star signs on the board. Ask what they are and what horoscopes talk about. Elicit or teach *future*. You could get students to brainstorm related vocabulary in groups and use the words to write sentences. Students saw a personality test in Unit 4, so this is an opportunity to recycle adjectives of personality, and to teach *shy, interesting* and *lucky*, which are in the presentation text in the unit.

Student's Book answers

1b future
2a 1 is going to come
　　2 aren't going to have
　b 1 You aren't going to have any free time.
　　2 You're going to be busy.
　　3 You are going to have a good week.
　　4 You aren't going to have a bad week.
3 1 Paulo's dad is going to open the window.
　　2 The cat is going to jump on the table.
　　3 Paulo's brother/Carlos is going to kick the cat.
　　4 Paulo's sister is going to eat some/the chocolates.
　　5 Paulo's mum is going to answer the phone.
　　6 Paulo is going to go out.
4 1 She's going to throw the ball.
　　2 He's going to catch the ball.
　　3 They're going to drop the plates.
　　4 It's going to break.
　　5 They're going to fall in the river.

▶ *Worksheet*

Classwork suggestion

Students mime to the class the verbs in exercises 3 and 4 but stop short of performing the action. Ask students to think of different objects, e.g. *open the door; kick the ball*. The class says what they're going to do.

Groupwork suggestion

In groups, students write sentences with *going to* about five actions which need lots of preparation, e.g. *going to go on holiday*, which needs packing bags, etc. or *going to drive a car*, which needs opening the door, getting in, putting seat belt on, checking mirrors, turning the ignition key, etc. Groups mime their preparation to the class who guess the marker sentence. This is an opportunity to practise the present continuous for naming the preparing actions, e.g. *He's packing his bag, He's opening the door*, etc. You could do this activity as a competition, with points given to the group who guesses the sentence first.

Student's Book answers

5 1 They aren't going to come.
　　2 He isn't going to ride his bike/it.
　　3 He isn't going to get up.
　　4 She isn't going to eat (the) sausages/them.
　　5 They aren't going to do their homework.
6 1 He's going to wash his dog on Saturday.
　　2 He's going to take his bike to the bike shop on Saturday.
　　3 He's going to write to his grandma on Sunday.
　　4 He's going to meet Sue on Sunday.
　　5 He's going to do his music project on Sunday.

Classwork suggestion

Tell students to write an ideal (the things they would like to happen most) prediction for next week, using the presentation texts in exercise 1 as models. (You can set this writing as homework if there is not enough time in class.) Collect all the papers and put them in a bag. Each student pulls out a piece of paper which becomes their prediction. They should read it and try to make any corrections to the English before reading it out to the class.

Student's Book answers

7 Answers will vary.

Puzzle

Yes – it's this boy's party, or his brother's.

Worksheet

Extra vocabulary: *close, hit*

Use this activity after exercise 4 for vocabulary practice and extension. Preteach *close* (as the opposite of *open*) and *hit*; mime is a good idea. Students then do the activity.

Answers　1 open*ing*　2 catch　3 drop*ping*　4 hit　5 fall*ing*
　　　　　　6 break*ing*　7 throw　8 close　9 jump*ing*　10 kick

Look at the pictures. Then complete the sentences with the words below.

break   catch   close   drop   fall   hit
jump   kick   open   throw

THE TERRIBLE TENNIS MATCH

Kate's having a bad day, and she's going to play tennis …

1 She's _____ing her bag.

2 She's going to _____ the ball.

3 No! She's _____ing the ball.

4 She's going to _____ the ball.

5 No! She's _____ing over!

6 She's _____ing her racket!

7 She's going to _____ the ball!

8 She can't _____ her bag

9 She's _____ing on her bag!

10 She's going to _____ her bag!

20 What are you going to watch?

Be going to questions and short answers

Meaning
In this unit, *be going to* has the same three uses as in Unit 19. In exercises 4 and 5, *going to* is used to talk about the weather. To predict weather conditions, *going to* and *will* are often used interchangeably. (Impersonal *it* is used in these exercises for the first time.)

Form
Questions with *going to* are made by inverting the subject and auxiliary *be*; *going to* and the main verb don't move. Short answers use only the auxiliary *be*.

Vocabulary
Nouns: *east, horror film, line, north, part, programme, size, south, tomorrow, weather, weather man, weather map, west*
Verbs: *rain, snow*
Adjectives: *cloudy, same, sunny*

Preview suggestion
Ask students if they watch TV, how many hours' TV they usually watch a day and what they like watching on TV.

Student's Book answers
1b Nature Watch   The Thing 3
2a 1 Is he going to watch TV?
   2 Are they going to watch TV?

b
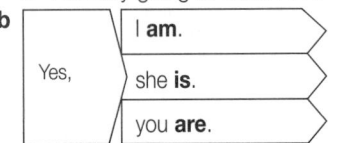
Yes, I am. / she is. / you are.

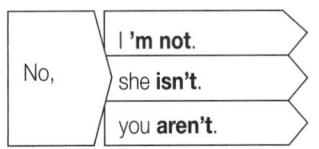
No, I 'm not. / she isn't. / you aren't.

3 1 d 2 e 3 a 4 b 5 c
   1 Are they going to watch Nature Watch?
   2 Is he going to do his homework?
   3 Is she going to go to the party?
   4 Are they going to do any sport next weekend?
   5 Are you going to fly to Turkey?
4 1 It's going to be cloudy in the east.
   2 It's going to rain in the west.
   3 It's going to snow in the north.
   4 It's going to be sunny in the south.
5 1 Is it going to be cloudy in the east?
      No, it isn't. It's going to be sunny.
   2 Is it going to rain in the west?
      No, it isn't. It's going to be cloudy.
   3 Is it going to snow in the north?
      No, it isn't. It's going to rain.
   4 Is it going to be sunny in the south?
      Yes, it is.

▶ Worksheet A

Student's Book answers
6 1 Where are you going to go?
   2 When are you going to go?
   3 Who are you going to go with?
   4 What are you going to do?

▶ Worksheet B

Pairwork suggestion
Bring in TV/radio guides for the week ahead and make copies to give to pairs. Students ask each other questions, e.g. *What are you going to watch on Monday? Are you going to listen to the baseball match on Wednesday?* They then tell the class what their partner is going to do in the coming week.

Student's Book answers
7 Answers will vary.
Puzzle

Worksheet

Extra vocabulary: *cloud, fog, foggy, rainy, snow(n), snowy, wind*

A Use this activity after exercise 5 for vocabulary practice and extension. Elicit the words from the pictures that students know and preteach *wind, fog*. The spelling rule for adjectives ending in one vowel + one consonant is that the final consonant doubles; e.g. *fog – foggy*. Elicit or point out that the rule is similar to the *-ing* spelling rule. Students do the activity for consolidation and written record.
   Answers 1 cloud, cloudy   2 fog, foggy   3 rain, rainy, rain
      4 snow, snowy, snow   5 sun, sunny   6 wind, windy

B Use this activity after exercise 6 for vocabulary practice and extension. Students do the activity.
   Answers Possible words: bag, ball, beach, bin, boy, burger, camera, chair, chips, cup, dog, donkey, girl, hat, ice cream, litter, man, sea, sky, sun, sun cream, sunglasses, towel, woman

   Extension suggestion Students write sentences about the scene. This is an opportunity to recycle most of the grammar from previous units.

What are you going to watch?

A Complete the chart for the weather words.

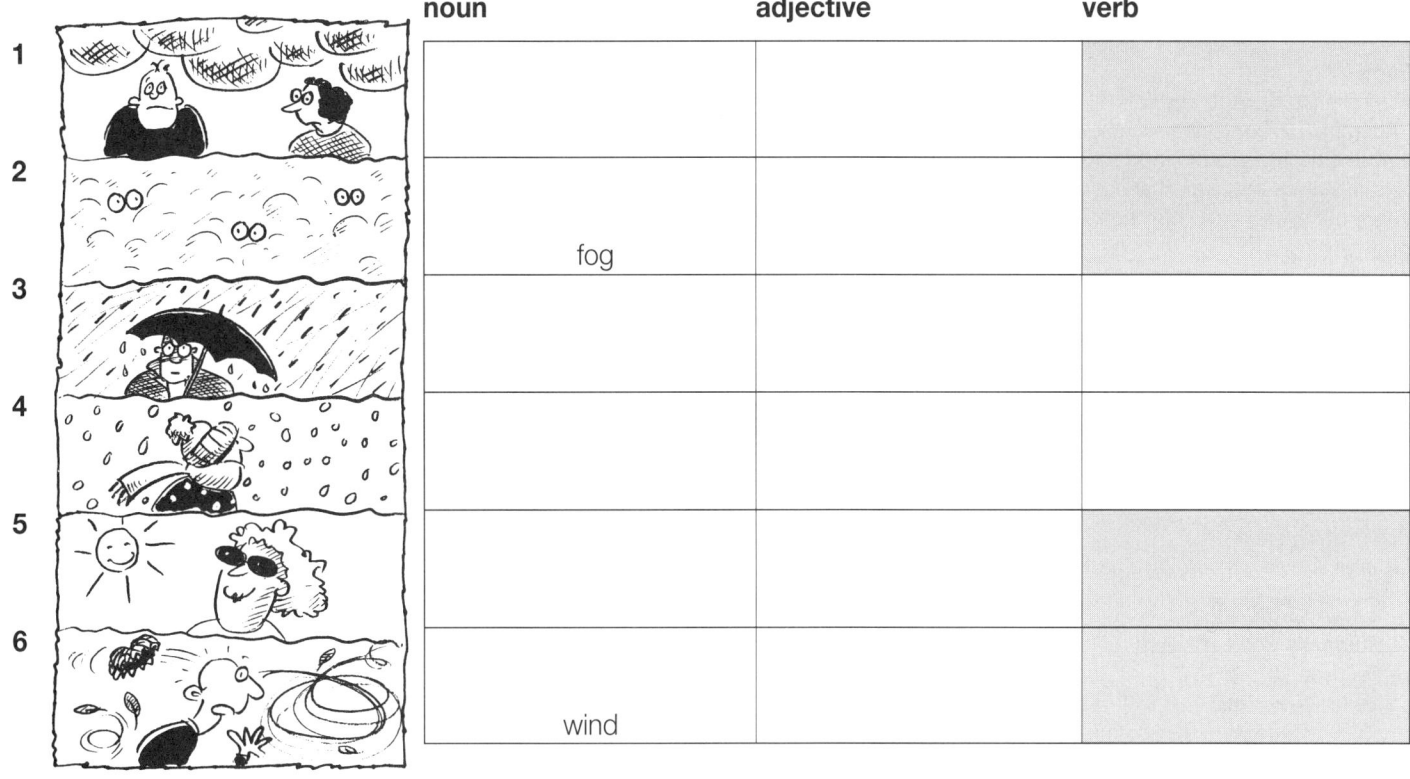

	noun	adjective	verb
1			
2	fog		
3			
4			
5			
6	wind		

B Look at the picture of the beach. How many things do you know?
Write the words and draw arrows (→) to the things.

10 = good
14 = very good
18 = excellent

Be past tense

Meaning

The past tense of *be* refers to ongoing or temporary states in the past. These can be recent or in the distant past.

Form

• Unlike the present tense of *be*, the past tense of *be* has no contracted form in the affirmative.

• In the negative, contractions are made with *not* (*n't*) rather than with the subject, and are usually used in spoken English. Contractions are not usually used in written English except in informal texts.

Pronunciation

The weak forms /wəz, wə/ are usually used. The strong forms /wɒz, wɜː/ are only used for emphasis. In short answers, the strong form is used because the verb is stressed.

Vocabulary

Nouns: *brain, hunter, metal, place, scientist, statue, wonder, world*
Verbs: *call, mean, was, were*
Adjectives: *ancient, hairy, handy, late, metal, small, snowy, thick, useful*
Adverb: *ago*
Determiner: *million*
Ordinals: *fourth, second, third, last*

▶ *Worksheet* **A** and **B**

Student's Book answers

1b past
2a is – was   isn't – wasn't   are – were   aren't – weren't
 b 1 Where were they from?
   2 They were from Africa.
   3 Were they tall?
   4 No, they weren't.
3 1 She was 2 It was 3 She wasn't 4 There weren't
   5 She was

Groupwork suggestion

Play a memory game. Bring different common objects to class (which students know the names of in English) and place them on a table at the front of the class. Allow students to look at the objects for a given time, e.g. one minute, and then get students to turn round or put up a screen with a cloth or newspaper and change the arrangement, by putting things in different places, removing some things and adding others. In their groups, students have to write sentences using *was/were* and *is/are*, e.g. *The pen was next to the pencil. Now it is next to the cup*. Groups get points for remembering the individual objects and for correct grammar. For speaking practice, students can play this game amongst themselves in small groups using items out of their school bags.

Student's Book answers

4 1 Was it 2 Was it 3 Was it 4 Were they 5 Were they
   6 Were
5 1 Yes, it was.
   2 Yes, it was.
   3 No, it wasn't.
   4 No, they weren't.
   5 Yes, they were.
   6 Yes, they were.

6a 1 What was the Colossus?
   2 Who was Cleopatra?
   3 What was the Titanic?
   4 Who were the Wright brothers?
   5 Who was Martin Luther King?
   6 What were the Hanging Gardens?
   7 Who was Amelia Earhart?
 b 1 The Colossus: see exercises 4 and 5.
   2 Cleopatra was a queen of Ancient Egypt at the time of Julius Caesar.
   3 The Titanic hit an iceberg on its first voyage across the Atlantic in April 1912. The ship sank and 1,513 people died.
   4 The Wright brothers (Wilbur and Orville) flew the first aeroplane in December 1903.
   5 Martin Luther King was an American black civil rights leader. He died in 1968.
   6 The Hanging Gardens: see exercises 4 and 5.
   7 Amelia Earhart was, in 1928, the first woman to fly across the Atlantic. Her plane disappeared over the Pacific in 1937.
7 Answers will vary.

Pairwork suggestion

Students practise asking and answering the questions in exercise 7 in pairs.

Student's Book answers

Puzzle

1st = Number 2; 2nd = Number 7; 3rd = Number 18;
4th = Number 9

▶ *Worksheet* **C** and **D**

Worksheet

Extra vocabulary: *fifth, hour, minute, yesterday* + numbers

A and **B** Use these activities as a preview to the unit. Elicit or preteach the new words for activity B: *yesterday, last (week), (two days) ago*. (You could use a timeline on the board.) Students do activities A and B.

Answers A a minutes, hour b hours, day c days, week
   d months, year e weeks, year
   B 1 past 2 future 3 last week 4 this week
   5 next week 6 today 7 yesterday 8 tomorrow
   9 one week ago 10 two days ago

C and **D** Students do these activites for vocabulary practice and extension at the end of the unit.

Answers C a hundred 100 a million 1,000,000
   a thousand 1,000 eight 8 eighteen 18 eighty 80
   eleven 11 fifteen 15 fifty 50 five 5 four 4
   fourteen 14 forty 40 nine 9 nineteen 19 ninety 90
   one 1 seven 7 seventeen 17 seventy 70 six 6
   sixteen 16 sixty 60 ten 10 thirty 30 three 3
   thirteen 13 twelve 12 twenty 20 two 2
   D fifth = b first = e fourth = a last = c
   second = f third = d

Extension suggestion Write the answers for activity C on the board and ask students to say the numbers in English.

A Complete the sentences. Use the words below.

day   hour   ~~minute~~   month   week   year

a 60 ___minutes___ = 1 _____ .

b 24 _____ = 1 _____ .

c 7 _____ = 1 _____ .

d 12 _____ = 1 _____ .

e 52 _____ = 1 _____ .

B Put the words below on the diagram.

future   last week   next week   one week ago   ~~past~~   this week   today   tomorrow   two days ago   yesterday

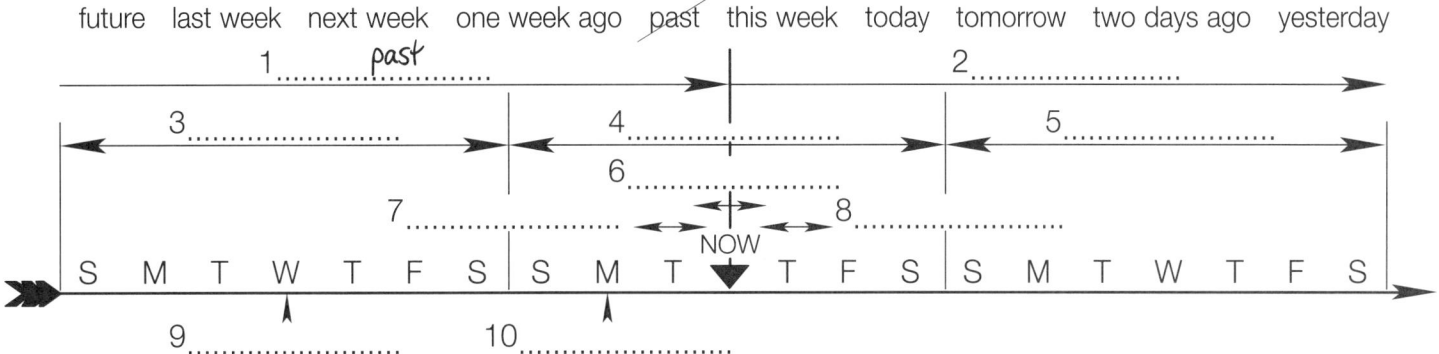

C Match the numbers with words.

a hundred	90	**18**	ninety
a million	1	70	one
a thousand	**8**		seven
eight		80 **100**	seventeen
eighteen	7	1,000,000	seventeen
eighty	**5**	11	seventy
eleven		16	six
fifteen	**15**	1,000 3	sixteen
fifty	**10**	6 **17**	sixty
five			ten
four	**30**	12	thirty
fourteen	4	**60**	three
forty		20	thirteen
nine	50	40 14	twelve
nineteen	9	2	twenty
	19	**13**	two

D Match the words below with the runners.

fifth   ☐

first   ☐

fourth   ☐

last   ☐

second   ☐

third   ☐

Past simple regular verbs   affirmative and negative

Meaning
The past simple is used for states or actions in the past.

Form
In negatives, where *don't/doesn't* is used in the present simple, *did/didn't* is used in the past simple and the main verb remains in the infinitive.

Spelling
Words ending in:

1 -y: -y + -ie + -ed   stud**ied**, carr**ied**
2 -e: + -d   like**d**, love**d**
3 a vowel and then a consonant (for example: -ir, -op, -ip), double the consonant + -ed   stir**red**, stop**ped**
   Note that verbs ending in the consonants -w, -y or -x do not follow this rule and these consonants do not double (e.g. *showed, played, fixed*).
4 Other words: + -ed   start**ed**, look**ed**, watch**ed**

Pronunciation
The pronunciation of past simple regular verb endings depends on the final sound of the verb.

- When the final sound is /t/ or /d/, the ending is pronounced /ɪd/.
- When the final sound is voiced, /b, g, v, ʒ, z, dʒ, m, l, n, ŋ/, or a vowel sound, the ending is pronounced /d/.
- When the final sound is unvoiced, /k, f, p, tʃ, s, ʃ/, the ending is pronounced /t/.

Vocabulary
Nouns: *fireworks, Greeks, gun, mathematics, pasta, Portuguese, printing*
Verbs: *arrive, explore, invent, sail, stop*
Adjective: *different*
Places: *Africa, Europe, Middle East, North Africa, Pacific Ocean*
Other words: *about, over*

▶ *Worksheet* **A** and **B**

Student's Book answers
1b 1 ✓ 2 ✗ 3 ✗
2a past
  b do – did   don't – didn't   does – did   doesn't – didn't
  c 1 stopped 2 didn't stop 3 visited 4 didn't visit
3a start**ed** stop**ped** stud**ied** like**d**
  b carried loved wanted stirred

Extension suggestion
Write a list of other regular verbs on the board making sure that there are examples of all the different endings. Note that verbs ending in vowel + -y, -w, -x (e.g. *play, pray, show, snow, fix, tax, fax*) have not been practised so be sure to include examples of these. Students write the past simple forms and compare with a partner before class correction.

Student's Book answers
4 1 painted 2 studied 3 sailed 4 played

Project work suggestion
In groups, students choose a famous person. They find out about the person's life and write sentences using past simple and present tenses for a poster. They can use photos, pictures and drawings to illustrate their work.

Student's Book answers
5 1 They didn't study English. They studied science.
   2 They listened to music. They didn't listen to the radio.
   3 They lived in Asia. They didn't live in America.
   4 They visited Africa. They didn't visit Europe.
   5 They cooked rice. They didn't cook burgers.
   6 They invented fireworks. They didn't invent (the) TV.
6 1 lived 2 were 3 studied 4 sailed 5 didn't visit 6 enjoyed
   7 invented 8 didn't play

Pairwork suggestion
Students write sentences about other important inventions/inventors. This could be developed into project work where students make a class poster using pictures cut from magazines/newspapers with their written descriptions. If students' factual knowledge is limited, encourage them to use reference books to help. Alternatively they can ask you.

Student's Book answers
7 Answers will vary.

Puzzle
c walked across the Atacama desert – the first letter of the verb is the same as the first letter of the season.

▶ *Worksheet* **C**

Worksheet

Extra vocabulary: *island, ocean, valley*

A and B Use these activities as a preview to the unit. Preteach *invent/invention/inventor* then the nouns *pasta, printing, firework(s), gun(s)*. Students do activity A for consolidation. Then ask which country these inventions come from; write students' answers on the board. Students then read the text in the Student's Book to check their ideas.
Answers A 1 b 2 d 3 a 4 c
       B China

C Use this activity at the end of the unit for vocabulary practice and extension.
Answers 1 sea 2 island 3 valley 4 river 5 ocean
       6 forest 7 mountain 8 desert

Writing suggestion Students draw a route across the continent of South America in activity C. They then write a description of their fictional explorer's journey, beginning in the same way as the puzzle: *In ..... , ... sailed to ... . She/He ... .*

C Write the words under the pictures.

desert   forest   island   mountain   ocean   river   sea   valley

1.
2.
3.
4.
5.
6.
7.
8.

Caribbean
Amazon
Amazonia
Andes
Atacama
PACIFIC

A Match the words with the pictures.

1 fireworks ☐   2 guns ☐

3 pasta ☐   4 printing ☐

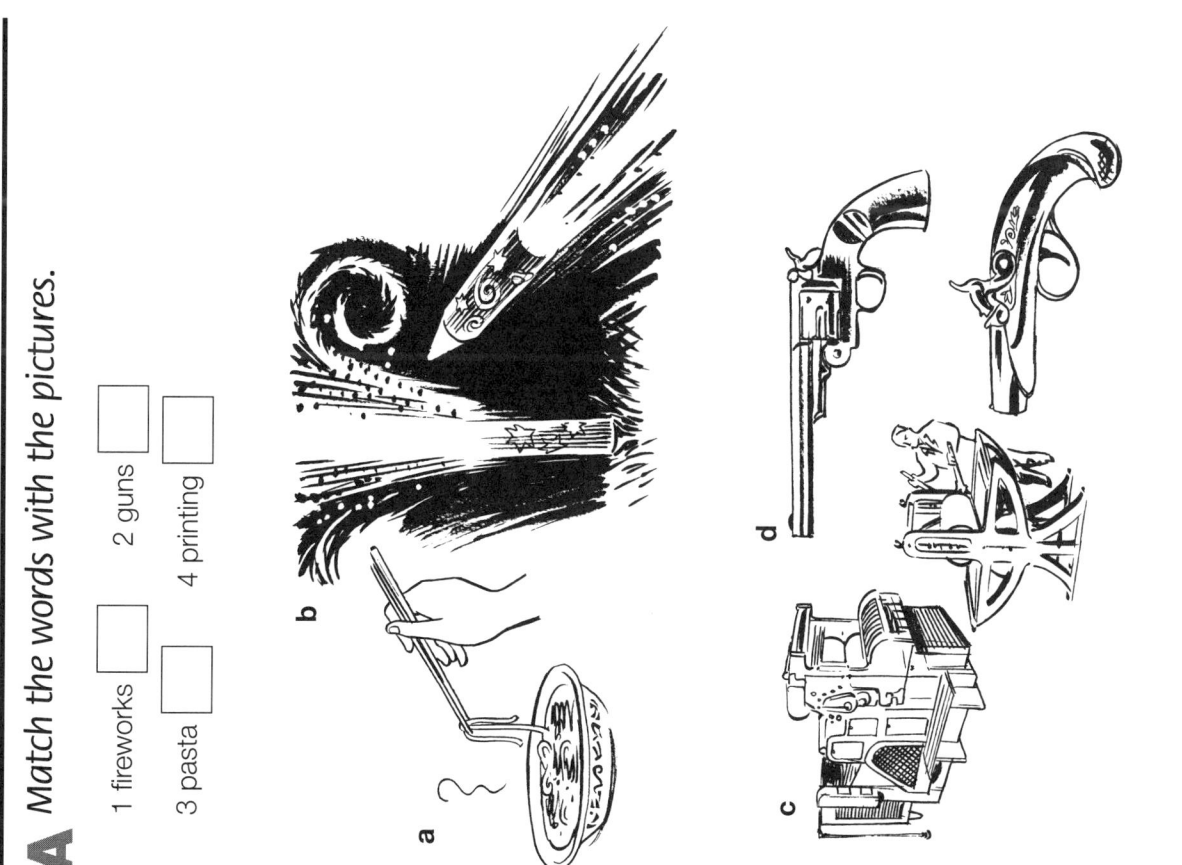

a

b

c

d

B Where do these inventions come from?
Can you name the country?

23 Aunt Flo visited us

Past simple   irregular verbs
Past simple   questions and short answers

Form

In questions, where *do/does* is used in the present simple, *did* is used in the past simple and the main verb remains in the infinitive.

Spelling

Encourage students to learn verbs with irregular past forms – there is no general guiding rule to predict the past form from the infinitive. Point out to students that question and negative forms of past simple with irregular verbs use *did/did not (didn't)* and verb infinitive like regular verbs.

Vocabulary

Nouns: *body, Egyptians, motorcycle, piece*
Verbs: *stay, tell*
Adjectives: *boring, sick*
Determiner: *hundreds*
Other words: *early*

Student's Book answers

1b 1 ✗ 2 ✓ 3 ✗
2 1 had 2 made 3 gave 4 ate 5 sat 6 told 7 sang
    8 drank 9 went

Groupwork suggestion

Class forms groups of about 5–6 students. All the students stand up. S1 says an irregular verb in its infinitive form and S2 says its past simple form and then another irregular verb infinitive. S3 says the correct past simple form and then another irregular infinitive, and so on. If a student gets the answer wrong or cannot think of an irregular past infinitive within a reasonable time, she/he has to sit down and is out of the game. (The winner from each group can then take part in a grand final competition.)

Student's Book answers

3 1 We went to the zoo.
   2 Carlos rode an elephant.
   3 We saw a gorilla.
   4 I gave it a banana.
   5 It threw the banana.
   6 Dad fell down!
4a 1 Did you have a good weekend? No, I didn't.
   2 Did she enjoy the weekend? Yes, she did.
b 1 When did she go?
   2 Where did they go?
   3 What did they see?
5 1 Did the Ancient Chinese eat rice?
    Yes, they did. They didn't eat chips.
   2 Did the Ancient Chinese drink tea?
    Yes, they did. They didn't drink coffee.
   3 Did dinosaurs have big bodies?
    Yes, they did. They didn't have big brains.
   4 Did Attila the Hun ride a motorcycle?
    No, he didn't. He rode a horse.
   5 Did Columbus go to Australia?
    No, he didn't. He went to America.

▶ *Worksheet* **A** and **B**

Group/Classwork suggestion

Set up a general knowledge quiz. Divide the class into groups of about three students. Each group writes three general knowledge questions about the past using *When, Where, Who, What, Did … ?* They take it in turns to read their questions to the class and the other groups discuss and write down the correct answers. At the end, answers are checked to find the winning group.

Student's Book answers

6 1 Who were these people?
   2 When did they live?
   3 Where did they live?
   4 What did they eat?
   5 What did they make?
7 Answers will vary.

Pairwork suggestion

Students ask their partner questions about what they did last weekend, e.g. *Did you study English?* etc. When they have asked all the questions, they can feed back to the class, e.g. *Elena didn't study English last weekend. She played tennis*, etc.

Writing suggestion

Students write about what they did on a special day in the past, e.g. last New Year, last Christmas, or another special day in your country. (Regular and irregular past simple verbs are acceptable here.)

Student's Book answers

Puzzle

There are three women: a daughter, a mother and a grandmother. The mother is also a daughter, as the grandmother is her mother.

Worksheet

A and B Use these activities to revise words for everyday objects after exercise 5.

Answers A a telephone   b (electric) guitar   c piano
          d telescope   e television   f car   g aeroplane
          h radio   i CDs   j jeans   k English dictionary
          l sandwich   m bike/bicycle   n stamps   o camera
          p watch
      B a = 2; b = 13; c = 4; d = 7; e = 1; f = 3; g = 16;
        h = 11; i = 12; j = 5; k = 9; l = 6; m = 10; n = 14;
        o = 15; p = 8

A Write words with the pictures.

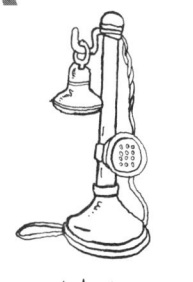

a ___telephone___ [2]

b _____ [ ]

c _____ [ ]

d _____ [ ]

e _____ [ ]

f _____ [ ]

g _____ [ ]

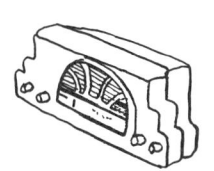

h _____ [ ]

i _____ [ ]

j _____ [ ]

k _____ [ ]

l _____ [ ]

m _____ [ ]

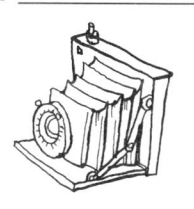

n _____ [ ]

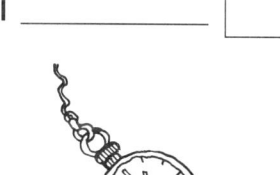

o _____ [ ]

p _____ [ ]

B Can you match the inventors below with the inventions in activity A?

1 Baird 1926

2 Bell 1876

3 Benz 1886

4 Cristofori 1690s

5 Davis and Strauss 1874

6 Earl of Sandwich 1718–1792

7 Galileo 1608

8 Huygens 1675

9 Johnson 1755

10 Macmillan 1840

11 Marconi 1901

12 Philips and Sony 1982

13 Rickenbacker 1932

14 Royal Mail 1840

15 Talbot 1835

16 Wright brothers 1903

Why ... ? ... because ...
How + adjective ... ?
What + object ... ?

Why/because: Meaning
Why and *because* refer to cause and effect relationships and students sometimes confuse these, e.g. * *I was hungry because I went to a restaurant.*

Form
In written English, a sentence with *because* should have two clauses, one for cause, one for effect. In spoken English, we often use *because* without the effect clause, e.g. *Why are you late? Because I missed the bus.*

How + adjective: Meaning
How + adjective questions can use any adjective which is appropriate to the context.

What + object: Form
What questions are not new to students but this is the first time the object has been explicitly included in the question, e.g. *What do you do? / What job do you do?* The object is usually dropped if it is clear from the context what the object is.

Vocabulary
Nouns: *block, block of flats, German, ground, horror story, medal, quiz, stairs, team*
Verbs: *miss, score*
Adjectives: *fifth, heavy, high, married, tenth*
Other words: *altogether, because, why*

Student's Book answers
1b 1 ✗ 2 ✗ 3 ✗
2b 1 c 2 a 3 b
  c Why are they running?
3 1 Why are you late?
  2 Because I missed the bus.
  3 Why did you miss the bus?
  4 Because I got up late.
  5 Why did you get up late?
  6 Because I woke up late.
  7 Why did you wake up late?
  8 Because I went to bed late.
  9 Why did you go to bed late?
  10 Because I watched the eclipse last night.

Pairwork suggestion
In pairs, one student imagines she/he is late and the other student asks questions in the same way as in exercise 3. Students should try to produce unusual reasons. The aim is to have as many question/answer exchanges as they can.

Student's Book answers
4a 1 d 2 b 3 c 4 a
  b How high is Mount Everest?
  d 1 What US team did he play for?
    2 How many teams did he play for?
5 1 How long was it?
  2 How heavy was it?
  3 How tall was it?
  4 How long were its teeth?

6 1 What languages does he speak?
    How many languages does he speak?
  2 What books do you read?/What books do you like reading?
  3 How many pets have you got?
    What pets have you got?
  4 What car does she drive?
  5 How many children have they got?
7 Answers will vary.

Groupwork suggestion
Play 'Name the Animal'. (See exercise 6 in *Check point* 19–24.) The class arranges itself into four groups. Each group chooses an animal, fish, insect or bird that they are able to answer questions about. (They could research details for homework or with encyclopaedias in class.) Then groups pair up and take it in turns to ask questions to guess the other group's animal, e.g. Group A questions group B *How big is it? How many legs has it got?* until they can guess the animal. Then group B questions group A in the same way. The number of questions it takes to guess the animal is recorded. Groups then change pairs (A + C and B + D) and repeat the procedure; then they change again (A + D and B + C) and repeat. The winning group is the one which has asked the lowest number of questions to guess all the animals. (Advise students to keep their voices down to avoid being overheard by other groups.)

Student's Book answers
Puzzle
Because the little boy is short – he cannot reach the button for the tenth floor.

▶ *Worksheet*

Worksheet

Extra vocabulary: *height, kilo, kilogram, kilometre, length, light, speed, weight*

A, B and C Use these activities at the end of the unit for practice and extension.
  Answers A 1 high 2 tall 3 big 4 small 5 heavy 6 light
      7 long 8 short 9 slow 10 fast
    B height, size, weight, length, speed
    C metres, metres/kilos (kilograms), kilos (kilograms), metres, kilometres per hour

A Look at the pictures. Write the letters below in the correct order. Put the words under **adjectives** in the chart in activity C.

1 h h g i   2 l a l t   3 g i b   4 l a l m s   5 v e h y a

6 g l i t h   7 n o l g   8 t h r o s   9 w o l s   10 s t a f

---

B Put the words below under **nouns** in the chart in activity C.

height   length   size   speed   weight

C Put the words below under **measurement** in the chart.

hour   metres   kilometres   metres   kilos (kilograms)   metres   kilos (kilograms)

		adjectives	nouns	measurement
1		1 _____		m = _____
2		2 _____		_____
3		3 _____		m/kg = _____
4		4 _____		_____
5		5 _____		kg = _____
6		6 _light_ _____		_____
7		7 _____		m = _____
8		8 _____		_____
9		9 _____	_speed_	kph = _____
10		10 _____		per _____

1 1 What's he going to do?
He's going to jump in the pool.
2 What's she going to do?
She's going to paint a picture.
3 What are they going to do?
They're going to play basketball.
4 What's he going to do?
He's going to take a photo.
5 What's it going to do?
It's going to eat the fish.

2 1 Is Sue going to cook the sausages and chicken?
2 Is James going to make the sandwiches?
3 Are Paulo and Carlos going to telephone our friends?
4 Am I going to tidy the house?

3 1 No, she isn't. She's going to make a cake.
2 No, he isn't. He's going to cook the sausages and chicken.
3 No, they aren't. They're going to make the sandwiches.
4 No, you aren't. You're going to telephone our friends.

4 carried   hated   ran
climbed   had   stayed
closed   invented   stopped
came   knew   studied
did   liked   thought
went   made   walked

5 1 weren't   2 dropped   3 broke   4 wasn't   5 was   6 threw
7 ran   8 ate   9 rained   10 went   11 watched   12 was
13 didn't have   14 are going to go

6 1 Where is it from? / Where does it live?
2 What (food) does it eat?
3 How big is it?
4 What colour is it?
5 How many legs has it got?

1 1 She's going to eat an apple.
2 He's going to read a newspaper.
3 It's going to rain.
4 He's going to ride his bike.
5 They're going to play football.
6 She's going to climb a tree.

2 1 Was he (in the room)?   Yes, he was.
2 Were they in the room?   No, they weren't.
3 Was she in the room?   No, she wasn't.
4 Were you in the room?   No, I wasn't.

3 1 She woke up late.
2 She didn't eat breakfast.
3 She broke her umbrella.
4 She didn't take the dog for a walk.
5 She ran to school.
6 It was Saturday!

4 1 Where   2 What   3 How   4 How many   5 Whose
6 Who   7 When/What time   8 How

1 Look at the picture. Write sentences with *going to*.

1 _____

2 _____

3 _____

4 _____

5 _____

6 _____

2 Write questions and short answers. Use the past tense of *be*.

1 *Was he* in the room?

Yes, _____ .

2 _____ ?

No, _____ .

3 _____ ?

No, _____ .

4 _____ ?

No, _____ .

3 Kim had a bad day yesterday. Look at the pictures and write affirmative or negative sentences with the past simple.

1 _____

2 _____ breakfast.

3 _____ umbrella.

4 _____

5 _____

6 It _____ Saturday!

4 Read the answers. Then complete the questions.

1 _____ do you live?   In Liverpool.

2 _____ do you do?   I'm a student.

3 _____ heavy is an elephant?   About 6 tonnes.

4 _____ _____ days are there in a week?   Seven.

5 _____ bag is this?   It's mine.

6 _____ invented the TV?   Marconi.

7 _____ do you get up?   At 7.00.

8 _____ do you make green?   Mix blue and yellow.